LOP RABBITS

as pets

SANDY CROOK

Acknowledgments

I want to thank the many people and Lops who helped formulate and make this book possible (you all know who you are)—especially Bruce Crook, Cherie Verber, Alene Eden, Sandee Rudolph and Jackie Ayers.

With Lops of Love,
Sandy

PHOTOS BY BRUCE CROOK

Front cover:
Tortoiseshell Senior English Lop doe, courtesy of Eden's Olde English rabbitry; Broken Madagascar Senior French Lop doe, courtesy of Crook's Lophouse; Frosty point Junior Holland Lop doe, courtesy of Five A Bouble Bar Bunny Ranch; Fawn Senior Mini Lop doe, courtesy of Hoppin' Posie Loppitry. Photo by Bruce Crook.

The text of the chapter about the health of Lop rabbits (pages 111 through 141) has been reviewed and approved by Francis H. Goldsmith, Jr., D.V.M. of Rancho Bernardo Veterinary Clinic, San Diego, California.

Distributed in the UNITED STATES by T.F.H. Publications, Inc., 211 West Sylvania Avenue, Neptune City, NJ 07753; in CANADA by H & L Pet Supplies Inc., 27 Kingston Crescent, Kitchener, Ontario N2B 2T6; Rolf C. Hagen Ltd., 3225 Sartelon Street, Montreal 382 Quebec; in ENGLAND by T.F.H. Publications Limited, 4 Kier Park, Ascot, Berkshire SL5 7DS; in AUSTRALIA AND THE SOUTH PACIFIC by T.F.H. (Australia) Pty. Ltd., Box 149, Brookvale 2100 N.S.W., Australia; in NEW ZEALAND by Ross Haines & Son, Ltd., 18 Monmouth Street, Grey Lynn, Auckland 2 New Zealand; in SINGAPORE AND MALAYSIA by MPH Distributors (S) Pte., Ltd., 601 Sims Drive, # 03/07/21, Singapore 1438; in the PHILIPPINES by Bio-Research, 5 Lippay Street, San Lorenzo Village, Makati Rizal; in SOUTH AFRICA by Multipet Pty. Ltd., 30 Turners Avenue, Durban 4001. Published by T.F.H. Publications Inc. Manufactured in the United States of America by T.F.H. Publications, Inc.

CONTENTS

PREFACE, 5
DISPOSITION OF THE LOP, 10
THE LOP AS A PET AND COMPANION ANIMAL, 16
THE FLOPPY-EARED THERAPIST, 26
ENGLISH LOP, 35
FRENCH LOP, 40
MINI LOP, 44
HOLLAND (NETHERLAND DWARF) LOP, 47
SELECTING YOUR LOP(S), 50
HANDLING, 53
HOUSING, 56
DIET, 66
GROOMING, 78
HOUSEBREAKING, 90
HARNESSBREAKING AND TRICKS, 102
SHOWING, 104
HEALTH, 111
MEDICATIONS, 142
BREEDING, 150
KINDLING, 171
CARE OF MOTHER AND YOUNG, 178
WEANING, 183
REBREEDING THE DOE, 184
TATTOOING, 184
PEDIGREES, 187
SHIPPING, 188
ZONING REGULATIONS, 190
INDEX, 191

The final chapter on the Lops can never be written, because we have just begun to discover the extent to which they contribute to the richness of our lives through companionship, as a hobby, by providing priceless therapy for physically or mentally disabled people or as loving, accepting partners for prisoners or other confined individuals. Regardless of the challenge presented to them, the Lops have consistently risen to meet the challenge, exceeding even our fondest expectations.

The Lops have led the way into a new frontier for the pet rabbit, away from the meat and fur stigma of the rabbit world, and will successfully continue to do so. Lop charisma is, promoting them to the ranks of often-chosen pet/companion animals. Enough cannot be said for or about them and what they have done for people. The saga of the lovable Lops is a never-ending one.

Congratulations to you on your interest in this unique, affectionate and delightful pet rabbit—the Lop! More affectionate than a cat, and less demanding and quieter than a dog, the Lop will gain not only *your* love and respect, but that of any dog or cat whose domain he enters. Remember, any rabbit can be a bunny, but it takes a very special one to be a PET!

Preface

I have written this book in an effort to make a better place in the world for the Lop and for people. Having been a dog and horse enthusiast all my life, and not a lover of rabbits, the following is an explanation of how I came to be known as the "Mother of the Lops" and the "Lop Lady of San Diego County."

In 1976 at the Southern California Exposition at Del Mar, I bought what I was told was the "closest thing to a dog in a rabbit"—a French Lop. In the months that followed, I found this to be true of my broken agouti buck named Flippin-A-Lop (Flip).

Flip lived in a hutch under a tree in the yard—but not peacefully, once he had his freedom playing with the chickens, geese, cats, and dogs. He demanded attention, displaying jealousy if I fed the horses before I fed him and gave him the kisses and hugs and tender words he craved. This French Lop was truly a clown and a very affectionate pet which warranted my calling him a "Lop," and not a "rabbit." The time had come to find him a deserving mate and breed him in order to share this lovable Lop with other people.

If someone had told me at that time that the day would come when a big part of my life would be dedicated to the French Lops housed in a 30-hole rabbitry known as "Crook's Lophouse," plus another Lop in the house with four dogs and three cats, I would not have believed it. Even though the Lop has brought so much joy to many, there are thousands of people who do not know this type of animal exists as a pet. That is what prompted my one-woman campaign in 1979 to promote the French Lop, King of the Fancy (a noncommercial specialty) to the public: appearing on television and in newspapers and magazines, walking my Lop on a harness in a park, conducting educational seminars at Pet Fairs, libraries, schools, and community functions, and appearing at shopping center grand openings. Newscasters and newspaper reporters adopted French Lops and shared their pets with the public through their news media, "Leo the Lop" children's books came into being in memory of a pet French Lop owned by the illustrator, and puppeteers and a toy manufacturer obtained my help to create a Lop rabbit. Inevitably, the indoor Lop training cage was created for the indoor pet.

My phone-mate features "Lucy Lop," my cartoon character and ambassador of good will, who sounds like a Chinese laundry lady but she gets the job done when no one else can talk in person. The Lops receive cards and I receive letters not only from people, but from the Lops themselves!

When 1980 was declared the "Year of the Domestic Rabbit," I declared it the "Year of the French Lop" what could be more domestic! Subsequently, I have made every year the "Year of the French Lop." In 1981, I wrote and published a much-needed reference manual, YOUR FRENCH LOP, was founding President of the San Diego County Lop Breeders Association, and Director for Southern California and Hawaii for the Lop Rabbit Club of America.

Due to a near-fatal accident in May of 1981, I took a sabbatical from some of my duties, but managed to carry on a two-day seminar on the French Lop from a wheelchair at the American Pet Show at the Anaheim Convention Center with an attendance of approximately 35,000 people.

As a living testimonial and proof of the human/animal bond and animal-assisted therapy, I returned to the American Pet Show in July, 1983, as a member of the Delta

APPMA, the American Pet Products Manufacturers Association, featured seminars on the Lop as a pet. These seminars were given by the author (lady to the left). (Below): Two Lops are better than one and are ideal pets for the TV addict.

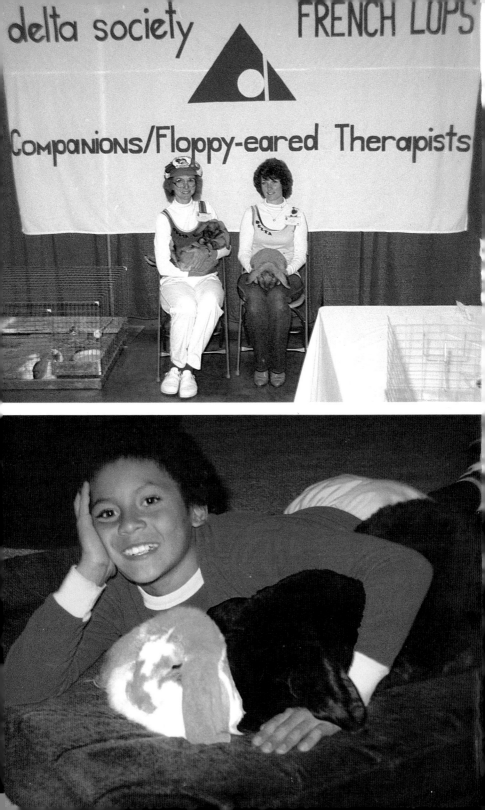

Preface

Society, telling of the "floppy-eared therapist" in animal-assisted therapy and human/animal bond with this companion animal that I love so very much.

In Genesis, the Lord said, "It is not good for man to be alone; I will make a companion for him, a helper suited to his needs." So the Lord God formed from the soil every kind of animal and bird, and brought them to Man to see what he would call them; and whatever he called them, that was their name. Today we are seeing the importance of the human/animal bond and recognizing the blessing that animals are today.

As Chief Sealth of the Duwamish tribe in Washington State observed in the 1850's: "What is a man without beasts? If all the beasts were gone, men would die from great loneliness of spirit, for whatever happens to the beast also happens to man. All things are connected. Whatever befalls the earth befalls the son of the earth."

I thank God for my animals and the opportunity to share the Lop with you.

Two floppy-eared therapists posing for their portraits. These animals are so docile and tranquil that using them as models is not very difficult. They are available in many colors, too, and they make better pets for home-bound people than do dogs or cats.

Disposition of the Lop

In the rabbit world, there are many breeds that fall into three categories: meat, fur and fancy. Lops are not a meat or fur breed. They are exclusively the fancy or pet breeds.

Lop babies, known as kittens or kits, will inquisitively and affectionately come to you, whereas other breeds generally will run away in fright like mice. Between the sixth and seventh week, the bonding of the kits is transferred from "mother" to humans; therefore, the earliest age for the adoption of a Lop as a pet should be seven weeks of age.

There is no ideal age of Lop with regard to adopting one as a pet. Lops are eager to please and therefore easily housebroken, taught to come when called, walk on a harness at the end of a leash, beg, play ball, jump through a hoop and live in harmony with other pets such as birds, cats, and dogs. Lops are clean and quiet and sometimes allowed in apartments where cats and dogs are prohibited. It has been said that older Lops train faster because they are more mentally mature. I believe that you will know the Lop you want as a pet when you see and hold him or her.

The Lops are choosy also. It is for this reason that I allow prospective owners to hold and spend time with the available Lops. I have seen a young Lop totally reject one family and a couple of hours later show great fondness for another family. There has to be mutual admiration. Lops reflect their owners and the feelings shown towards them. For instance, there was a couple that wanted a pet Lop. The husband wanted the chinchilla colored Lop and the

Even a star like Casey (being held by TV star Veronica Hamel) can be camera shy! (Below): Something for everybody. This group of kids discovers that Lops are a lot more fun than dogs (and they don't have to be walked so much!).

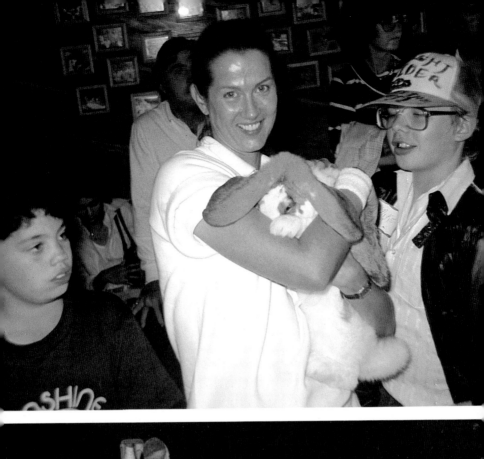

Disposition of the Lop

wife wanted the black. The chinchilla Lop went home with them, but much to the wife's dismay. They really never got along because of the resentment with regard to the color. The Lop sensed the wife's adverse feelings, took it personally and rebelled. The situation was corrected when the black Lop replaced the chinchilla. Now everyone's happy, including the chinchilla Lop who found a secret admirer.

The lovable Lop can become an unwanted third party, which is what happened to a pair of newlyweds who shared their apartment with a Lop. The wife spent much time training and loving the newest family member. The husband was not ready to share his new wife's time and affection and so hostile feelings were present, which surfaced when the Lop refused to be held by the husband.

Lops are very demonstrative and welcome indestructible, audible toys such as an empty soda pop can taped shut with a couple of stones placed inside.

They reflect their environment and do not do well shut in or placed by themselves. Known as the lovers of the rabbit world, they have been known to become lonely to the point of going off feed and even dying of a broken heart. Lops thrive on attention and the activity around them. A Lop is an animal that is always tuned in to your moods and feelings and the environment; thus you can see a reflection of yourself by observing your Lop.

Though generally happy-go-lucky, personable clowns, the Lops have been known to display jealousy and be discriminating in their choice of people and even mates.

Cyrano proves the need for resident pets to brighten convalescent and long term in-patient hospitals. (Below): Stephanie and the author meet Casey, the floppy-eared therapist. Patients like Stephanie find "You're Nobunny 'til Somebunny Loves You."

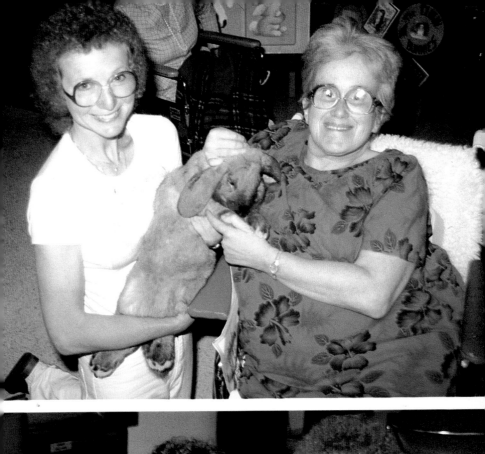

Disposition of the Lop

One Lop owner was truly baffled over her good pet's abnormal behavior when he started urinating at the foot of her bed. She admitted to having had a very busy schedule over the previous three weeks with out-of-town guests who had taken up all of her time. It seems the problem was no coincidence and started at the time her attention and time was taken away from her jealous companion.

Primitive instincts are seen in various situations of even the most domesticated pet Lop and also may be the reason for unusual behavior. I can recall a day at the park with Cyrano, a French Lop buck who thrives on public attention and walks on a leash. Cyrano froze in a crouched position when placed on the grass and resisted all attempts to move him. I looked around to see what could be the problem and even considered the fact that he might have been sick or even in a bad mood. Changing locations did not help nor did any amount of coaxing. Then remembering to think like a rabbit, which was so very well described by R. M. Lockley in his survival book series, *The Private Life Of A Rabbit,* I looked up and found the answer—kites! In the eyes of a Lop nothing is like the shadow of a hawk circling for its prey!

In short, the Lop has a mind and feelings.

Lops get along well with most other pets that are normally kept in your home. I call this Lop "Peewee." (Below): The Boston Terrier pup seems to get along amazingly well with Peewee even though Peewee is so much larger.

The Lop As A Pet And Companion Animal

Not many people have had a really true pet experience with a Lop and, therefore, not many people can ever imagine the love I have for my Lops and the reasons for it. The Lops are easily taught, controlled, and managed or cared for by children as well as adults of all ages and in some cases make better pets than a cat or dog. The following true experiences of mine since the Lophouse began may be of interest to you and will demonstrate the human/animal bond with regard to the Lop as a pet and companion animal.

My first French Lop, Flip, was sold at two years of age to a family with young children and two German Shepherd-type dogs. Flip played in the yard with the dogs, learned to scratch at the back door to be let into the house, slept with the young boy, swam in the pool with the family and went on to win a blue ribbon at a show.

A mother bought a young buck to be a house pet for her little girl and to live in her daughter's bedroom and found that the Lop was the best therapy ever for her hyperactive child. The Lop provided the child with a much-needed "quiet time," thereby allowing her to function in a more "normal" manner, even when separated from her pet.

A recently divorced woman found that her pet Lop provided the peace, tranquility and affection to help her cope with life.

A 3-month-old broken fawn Holland Lop buck in the "ugly" stage between 10 and 16 weeks of age when its ears are too narrow and the head is too large for the body. (Below): she sleeps with live dolls.

Lop As A Companion

A retired couple adopted a young doe for a house pet and traveled from California to Florida with her. I received a call to the effect that the wife had had a stroke and was bedridden for a week. The doe was in her bed loving her and licking her throughout that period. Also, the couple lost two close family members and felt that if it were not for the love of their pet Lop, they would not have been able to endure their hardships. They stated that all elderly people should have Lops. Now, using the breeder Lops they requested I ship to them they are filling orders from their friends.

One lady keeps her family Lop outside in a hutch and brings him in to play with the family. The Lop nudges her leg to be let out like a dog. Once, for attention, the Lop stole her pen from her hand and ran through the house with her pen in his mouth. After she retrieved her pen, he began chasing her through the house. Now it is a game.

Another lady living by herself in a condominium felt she had nothing to come home to until she brought home a black Lop rabbit to share her life with, and has since written and published short stories and poems about her beloved pet.

A bachelor I know of has found great kinship with a pet Lop buck who shares his suite, love for the TV, beer and snacks while lying across his master's chest in the evening.

A man who has a high-pressure job making life and death decisions at the D.A.'s Office found loving his pet Lop buck better than any martini or aspirin after a hard day's work; he recommends the same to all his co-workers, and believes a Lop should be on the staff to improve morale!

Lops can be very tolerant of other animals, but you must be careful that wild animals such as "stray" cats and wild rats do not infest your pet Lops with fleas or disease. The kitten and sable albino rat shown here are also housepets, so there isn't too much to worry about.

Lop As A Companion

After a transracial adoption, the ice was broken when a very withdrawn young black boy identified with a big black French Lop buck who came to live with him.

Chimps are not the only companions for truckers; there is a trucker sharing his cab with a French Lop buck—"Have Lop, will travel!"

Another traveler is a French Lop doe who met the requirements of a couple wanting a pet to share their tent as they toured the United States all hardy vegetarians and nature lovers.

Several couples swear their Lops are better than any dog or cat or bird they have ever had as a pet.

A teacher has her Lops not only for personal pleasure at home, but uses them for helping to teach the mentally and physically handicapped children in her classes.

A college student vegetarian who roomed with an exotic plant fancier found a pet Lop doe who not only was a fellow vegetarian but also was a lover of exotic plants who would never think of including one in her diet.

There are pairs of French Lops, one or both of which have been neutered, that are house pets. One pair has their own bedroom with bunny wallpaper, curtains and other bunny decor. They are the only kids, and Annie was adopted after Looie only for companionship for Looie because the mistress of the house returned to work—as an interior designer. Needless to say, Looie appreciates Annie's company, but prefers human companionship whenever possible. This is obvious to Annie because Looie's rapid departure means the return home of their master and mistress.

(Top, left): Four carrier cages are easily carried on a kennel cart. (Top, right): Peewee resting after his daily mail run. (Bottom): A group of California Lop enthusiasts formed a Holland Lop club.

Lop As A Companion

Another pair of French Lops share an outdoor pad on a patio. Thumper, being the first, does not mind showing Peggy how he likes to have things done or sharing his personal belongings, like food bowls or potty box. But Peggy sits in the box like a queen on a throne which evokes a big thump and push from Thumper–when a king's got to go, no one's allowed on the throne! Needless to say, Peggy runs. But chivalry is not dead as Thumper also digs a hole in the garden for Peggy to sleep in on hot days, before hopping off for his own nap in their den.

Steve McQueen had pet French Lops which kept a smile on his face even when hospitalized during his last days.

Maurice Lapin is a French Lop who has starred in a CHIPS series and has more debuts scheduled.

TV's "Grizzly Adams" stars a big Lop buck.

A pair of my French Lops reside as pets in the two-story house on the beach sometimes seen in the T.V. programs "Hawaii Five-O" and "Magnum, P.I." and share the house with many other pets off screen.

The absolute proof of the remarkable personality of the French Lop was made known to me several years ago when a woman who runs a slaughter house called me with the question as to what I do with my culls. The answer is that I do not have many culls, which was the reason for taking great care in selecting good, healthy foundation stock. The fact of the matter was that this lady, who butchers all types of animals for a living, could not find the heart to slaughter what, to her, were like little dogs, and therefore found homes for the French Lops (soul food)!

As new laws are passed, cities get more crowded, the economy gets worse, jobs get scarce, pressures mount and computers and television become a way of life devoid of

(Top, left): When preparing to kindle, a doe will clean the hay for her nest. (Top, right): This lilac Mini Lop is an example of a double dilute color. (Bottom): A broken blue Mini Lop junior buck. This is an example of dilute color, but the pattern is not desirable.

Lop As A Companion

another living thing, there is an increase in crime and loneliness. Society is making a big mistake prohibiting pets in apartments and other dwellings. There could be less crime, as pets remedy these ailments because of the human/animal bond, which attributes much to the mental health and physical well-being of people.

There is a pretty and very talented young women who is alive today because, when her whole world fell apart, she could not take her life and leave her pet French Lop doe. It was her bond to her pet that kept her going until the Lord reached her through a dream. Now, Karen and Honey Bun share their story and help reach people through F-E-A-T (Floppy-Eared-Animal-Therapy) programs (Delta Society) here in Southern California using French Lops as companion animals and as Floppy-eared Therapists. Need I say more?

The color of a Lop has little to do with its inherent pet qualities, though the more normal colors, having been inbred for so much longer than the rarer breeds, seem to have developed better personalities along the way. Rare colored Lops usually have been color bred rather than bred for a winning personality.

The Floppy-Eared Therapist
(The Human/Animal Bond)

Studies are proving the profound therapeutic and psychological value of the bond between humans and animals. The Lops have successfully come to be known as "Therapists with Floppy Ears," providing a bridge for communication between patient and experts in the healing professions, medical doctors, psychiatrists, psychologists and rehabilitation therapists. Encouraged by reports in medical journals, some doctors and therapists are routinely prescribing the presence of animals for patients, and several hospitals and other institutions have added resident pets which have brought about significant breakthroughs for the patients in animal-assisted therapy.

In 1975, in Lima State Hospital for the Criminally Insane in Ohio, there was decreased violence, improved morale of staff and patients and improved level of trust when resident pets were introduced. In a similar ward without pet therapy, there were higher incidences of suicide attempts and violence and higher requirements for medication.

In 1981, Ken White, Education Coordinator of The San Francisco SPCA, formerly a teacher of emotionally and educationally disadvantaged children with learning disabilities and behavioral problems, decided it best to place a resident animal at The Recreation Center for the Handicapped. The Center is an internationally respected facility in San Francisco providing day care therapy, recreation, education and socialization programs for more than

An automobile/bicycle accident victim in varying stages of recuperation. Although he was only mildly interested in the Lops in the beginning, they later became very close friends. The photos say it all, don't they?

The Floppy-Eared Therapist

1600 physically handicapped and mentally retarded adults and children. For reasons of size, temperament and habits, Ken and the Center's staff decided a rabbit would best suit their needs. The search began for the perfect bunny—one not too timid or too high strung to be happy in busy surroundings. In June of '81, a young albino Lop buck was taken to the Center. Nothing upset or distressed him. He was gentle and curious and loved everyone he met. The Lop was perfect.

Today, Bubba, the Floppy-Eared Therapist, is a resident animal on the staff of the Center, bringing much happiness and touching the lives of people in ways that nothing else could—helping and healing. Learning to care for Bubba has taught many of the people to care for themselves. It took three months for Mark to learn how to provide fresh water daily to Bubba because Bubba needs water to live, and Bubba depends on Mark to furnish it. What Mark learns about Bubba's care will help him comprehend things about himself and lead to a life of greater independence.

San Francisco University and the College of Veterinary Medicine, Washington State University, are two among a few educational institutions offering animal-assisted therapy programs for mentally, physically and emotionally handicapped individuals. Programs are springing up across the country and are in operation nationwide. Various colleges and universities include programs in animal-assisted therapy for health and social services professionals because animals are a bridge for communication between clients and health professionals. Conferences on the Human/Animal Bond are becoming more frequent around the world, i.e., the International Symposium on the Human-Pet Relationship held in Vienna, Austria, in October, 1983.

Four-month-old tortoiseshell (Madagascar) Holland Lop doe. (Below): French Lop broken steel doe with good body type.

The Floppy-Eared Therapist

In 1981, the Delta Society was formed. It is a non-profit professional association promoting the health and well-being of people and animals. Members conduct PSP (Public/Private School Partnership programs in libraries, schools and other institutions on animal awareness to promote respect and appreciation for all living things. Also there are PETE (Partnership in Equine Therapy and Education) programs and CAP (Companion Animal Partnership) programs which reach out to special people with special needs. These are all volunteer community programs.

In January, 1983, inspired by Ken White and the Delta Society, I joined the Society to establish programs here in San Diego County using the French Lops as companion animals and in educational and F-E-A-T (Floppy-Eared-Animal-Therapy) programs. The Lops have reached people that doctors, therapists, dogs and cats could not reach. What these animals have done for people is indeed a fantastic story.

The Lops are a motivating factor in the lives of people, providing exercise, serving as a social catalyst for communication with other people and serving as an important companion and confidant. They are uncritical, undemanding, significant beings that provide unconditional love.

People with learning and emotional problems better understand their own feelings and those of others, develop more responsible behavior, and a more positive self-concept through concrete experiences with a pet Lop. Two of my French Lops are residents in a transitional living facility and an important part of a program to help people break the cycle of returning to mental institutions and of helping to rebuild lives in society. One of the Lops has successfully

Steel Mini Lop senior doe posed for show. (Bottom): Holland Lop Siamese junior doe posed for judging.

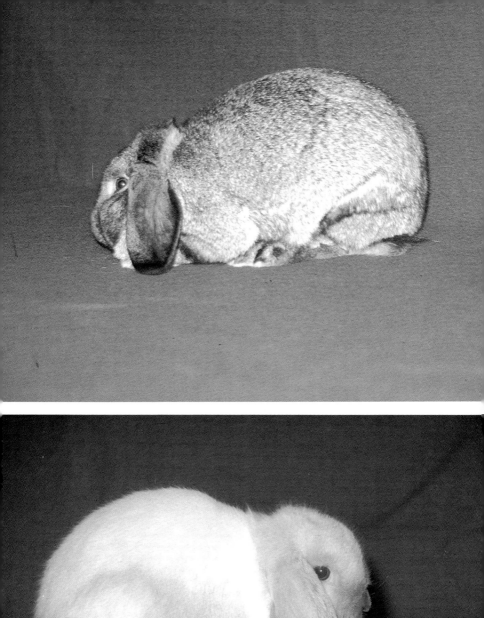

The Floppy-Eared Therapist

brought a young man out of a deep withdrawal and stabilized suicidal tendencies.

The Floppy-Eared Therapists and I work with rehabilitation therapists in various institutions and special schools dealing with the physically, mentally and emotionally handicapped and ill. The Lops uplift the human spirit and reach places in the human heart and mind which can be touched in no other way. We are part of the Sharp Hospital Rehabilitation Center Recreational Therapy program in San Diego, reaching the withdrawn, and motivating speech, laughter and movement when all else fails. In Beverly Manor Convalescent Hospital in Escondido, California, we have seen positive, loving behavior never before witnessed. One lady spoke, laughed, loved and cried while kissing and hugging my house Lop, Casey. We were later informed that she had been a resident there for eight months, exhibiting negative feelings and speaking not more than the same two words (and those, negative!) since her arrival. She had shown no response to programs using dogs and cats. Beverly Manor Convalescent Hospital now has a resident French Lop doe, Phebe, who has adjusted to life indoors just fine and has the run of the facility. Lop charisma works wonders!

Nursing homes encounter problems of loneliness, boredom, lack of sensory stimulation, depression and withdrawal. Visual stimulation through observing wild birds and fish does not satisfy the need for interaction in comparison to animal-assisted therapy and the human/animal bond. A resident Lop is the answer where human attention is difficult to provide—affording, as it does, visual stimuli and companionship, thereby

The two photographs on the facing page depict a very rare and recessive color. The Lop is a frosty point junior Holland Lop doe.

The Floppy-Eared Therapist

facilitating conversation, tactile stimulation and entertainment. A resident Lop is unconditional love and unconditional acceptance, and being clean and quiet, provides none of the negative qualities of some other domestic animals.

The Children's Mental Health In-Patient Program of Charter Oak Hospital (an 83-bed private psychiatric facility) in Covina, California, started raising Lops in 1983 for therapy. The entire staff admits to the success of the program and as a result, the bunnies will be residents of the facility for years to come.

Lops provide adoration, love, and approval, and enable people in all walks of life and of all ages to cope with reality. They have a boundless capacity for acceptance, attention and forgiveness. They are not a substitute for humans, but offer a different kind of relationship that augments and supplements human relationships.

THE FLOPPY-EARED THERAPISTS:
1. Decrease loneliness.
2. Are something to care for—a motivation—something to love.
3. Keep us busy.
4. Are something to touch, fondle and play with.
5. Are something to watch.
6. Make us feel safe.
7. Provide a stimulus for exercise.
8. Encourage more responsible, self-reliant behavior.
9. Reduce blood pressure for both person and animal.
10. Make us feel needed and cared about—loved.
11. Help us maintain a sense of humor.
12. Give self-esteem and a sense of achievement.
13. Correct helplessness—give independence.
14. Correct hopelessness.
15. Help maintain identity—a sense of self-worth.
16. Educate.

17. Are a social catalyst—widening the circle of warmth.
18. Increase cooperation with caregivers.
19. Help one cope with illness.
20. Increase life expectancy.
21. Reduce aggression and depression, which is a reaction to reality!

English Lop

HISTORY

Even though in the 16th century, European tapestries displayed large, gray rabbits with ears that lopped, it was not until the mid-1800's that the unique English Lop came into public view as a breed of Fancy rabbit. The English Lop is the oldest breed of domestic rabbit known to man and at one time the most successful throughout Europe.

In 1850, a Greater London Area newspaper featured George Powell's gray buck and black and white doe at the Chatham & Rochester Fancy Rabbit Club show with ears measuring 21 ¾ inches by nearly 5 inches and 21 ½ inches respectively. That same year, the first standard was drafted, allocating 25 points for ear length, 20 points for ear width, 5 points for ear carriage, 10 points for color and an equally-divided 20 points for eyes, weights, condition, size and shape.

In 1860, various types of Lops outside of the Natural Lop were classified as follows: Oar Lop—with ear carriage at 45 degrees and ears rising with body movement, commonly the Flemish Giant types; Half Lop—with ears falling to one side; Horned Lop—with ears falling forward over the face and eyes; and Flat Lop—with ears going upwards from the ear base, forming a crown and sweeping down and forward.

With great emphasis on ears, young Lops were often inhumanely subjected to having their ears coated in molten wax and then tugged and massaged, thereby breaking blood vessels and tearing muscles. Some had lead weights tied or pegged to their ear tips prior to a show, while others luckily got by with a leather head harness consisting of a strap with two holes for the ears and laced under the chin—an American invention and used in Germany well into the next century. Later it was found that the unnatural pulling of the ears caused cranial and spinal deformities.

The November 16, 1863, issue of *Fur & Feather* illustrated on the cover "Fawn Lop, City Wonder. 'Longest eared rabbit living.' Owned by T. Wallace. Judge Jennings measured it 28 inches at Bath."

In England, Lops were highly valued and London was the center of Lop shows. This monopoly led to the breed's decline in popularity regardless of an August, 1883, report by the London Fancy Rabbit Society acknowledging the importance of the development of the lop-eared pets. Popular colors were black and white, blue, white, yellow, sooty-fawn and tortoiseshell.

Hutch and rabbitry designs were centered around the same principles as an oven or hothouse at 80° to 100° to encourage ear growth inasmuch as chilling temperatures inhibit ear growth. Corrugated iron was most commonly used with a coal, wood or manure-burning furnace in the center of the building. Individual wooden or metal cages were left uncleaned to generate warmth. There was much loss of condition because of these practices. Pasteurella (snuffles) and pneumonia were common in show animals because of environmental extremes from heated rabbitries to open air or hall shows and because of unsanitary conditions. This forced breeders to revert to more natural and proper management.

In 1901, Captain Youlton broke all records when exhibiting a fawn English Lop with ears measuring 30-1/8 inches by 7-3/8 inches in the 6-month-old class at Warminster.

English Lop

The *Book of the Lop*, published in 1902 and Bosworth's *Chat on Lops* published in 1940, both failed to place any significant details on body type, though it was understood the body should be low at the shoulder and nicely curved over the rump. Again, too much emphasis was placed on ear properties.

In 1910, the National Lop Club show at Leamington exhibited 94 English Lops. But by 1949, the English Lop's popularity was waning. The National English Lop Club membership now stood at 51 individuals. In 1952, there were only 12 English Lops entered at the Bradford Championship Show, the championship's smallest breed entry.

In 1959, the Lop Club membership dropped to 33 individuals. The National Lop Club united with the independent Southern Lop Club in 1968 to form the present National Lop Club of Great Britain and had a 1978/79 membership in excess of 133 individuals. The English Lop is again a consistent winner in open shows in Great Britain, generally averaging 75 to 200 entries.

It is rumored that a famous buck named Robin Hood was exported from England to the United States around the turn of the century for over $200.00, that a class of English Lops was exhibited at the 1869 Sacramento, California, State Fair, and that an American Lop Club was formed around 1948 by B.J. Mickewitx of Massachusetts. In 1948, a pair of sooty fawns was imported from England and sold to the University of Chicago for $500.00, which may have been an all-time high for a pair of rabbits in the United States. This was just the start of many imports from England and the European continent by breeders enjoying the rabbit shows both in the United States and Europe.

CHARACTERISTICS OF THE MODERN ENGLISH LOP

The English Lop usually stands or poses with its head down. Due to the enormous ear size, they are vulnerable to all kinds of maladies and prone to ear infections. Body heat loss is also a problem because of the ear size and the fine, silky coat, lacking a dense undercoat.

The English Lop is placid and receptive to human handling. Bucks have an intense sexual drive, and does are prolific, as they have been found to rear as many as eight to ten young. The breed thrives and appears to be more lively in 70°-80° weather. They do not have good footpad fur; therefore solid wood flooring with deep straw bedding for ear and foot protection is recommended.

It is understood that the width of the ears of the English Lop is very important as it is an indication of the length and width of the body. Therefore, the ears should show very good width and length and be well rounded at the ends. Ear length at three to four months is 90 percent of the mature length, but may not have good substance at this time. There is no crown or rise between the ears as in the French, Mini and Holland Lops.

Bucks have a longer ear measurement due to a wider head, whereas does are finer and have a narrow skull. Ear blemishes can be kept to a minimum by keeping the toenails clipped and taking measures to prevent frostbite by using high water crocks, straw, and wooden flooring or sitting boards.

Ear measurement should be made from tip to tip using a yardstick.

Age	Approximate Length	Age	Approximate Length
4 weeks	11-16½ inches	10 weeks	22½-23½ inches
6 weeks	16½-20 inches	14 weeks	24-25 inches
8 weeks	20½-22 inches	16 weeks	25-26 inches

With past emphasis on ears alone, the 14-20 pound body of the early 1900's became smaller and lacked substance, and the once unique King of the Fancy Rabbit of Europe is still trying to overcome the effects of the eccentric and inhumane treatment of their ancestors. There is much work to be done to improve body development, health and vigor.

English Lop

Today, the breeders' goal is the return of the 30-inch-eared, 20-pound animal of the early part of the century.

SHOW ROOM CLASSES AND WEIGHTS

Show room classes are divided into two separate color classes (broken and self or solid) and also divided by sex and age. Weight is taken into account when determining the proper class, regardless of age. Bucks and does not over 6 months old and not over 9 pounds are Juniors. Does 6 to 8 months old and not over 11 pounds and bucks 6 to 8 months old and not over 10 pounds are Intermediates. Does 8 months old and older and not under 10 pounds and bucks 8 months old and older and not under 9 pounds are Seniors.

ENGLISH LOP STANDARDS

Both the American Rabbit Breeders Association (ARBA) and the British Rabbit Council (BRC) have published official standards delineating the ideal English Lop Rabbit; rabbits in show competition are judged according to the degree to which they fulfill the model defined by the standard. The standards of both national associations are subject to modification from time to time, and new standards are published as required. Full standards can be obtained from the associations involved.

There are two varieties of the English Lop; solid or self colors and broken colors (colors broken by white). The colors within each variety are not judged separately: all solid colors are grouped together and the various broken colors are considered a separate group.

Good color, including conformity of eye color, is allowed 5 points out of a possible 100-point total for the English Lop.

General type is allowed 72 points. With head allowed 10 points and ears allowed 30 points, they outweigh the 25 points allowed for body. Together, feet and legs are given 5 points. The tail is given the minimum amount of 2 points.

Fur is allowed 5 points, markings 8 points and condition 10 points.

French Lop

HISTORY

Eighteenth century people became interested in breeding two types of rabbits: those with erect ears and those with lop ears, which were a mutation.

It is believed the first French Lop was bred in France in 1853 by M. Cordonnier, and was the result of crosses of the English Lop, Normandy Giant and Flemish Giant.

By October, 1869, a German breeder, Mr. Warner, with the assistance of Mr. Meyer, imported from Avignon, France, Lop rabbits weighing 19 pounds with 7 inch lop ears. In April, 1872, 16 more French Lops were imported from France by Messrs. Warner, Meyer and Hochstetter to meet the growing demand.

The Germans perfected the French Lop and have done much to promote the great stature so characteristic of the breed. It still remains the most popular German breed and enjoys popularity throughout Northwestern Europe, Italy, People's Republic of China and the United States, where it is King of the Fancy or "pet" rabbit.

The humorous antics of the French Lop have endeared them to many people all over the world and earned them the title of "the clown of the bunnies." They thrive on attention and love, aim to please, love to play with toys and have been known to die of a broken heart.

The December, 1948, issue of *American Small Stock Farmer* featured a pair of white French Lops owned by Herman Jaeggi of Davenport, Iowa. Regardless of their early debut in the United States, the public was not ready for them until the '70's, with the appearance of *"Leo the Lop"* children's books in 1979, dedicated to the memory of a French Lop. Stock was imported from Holland, Scotland, Belgium and Switzerland. In 1971, the Lop Rabbit Club of America was founded.

French Lop

In 1960, many imports arrived in England, where the French Lop began to take hold like the English. The French Lop exceeds the English in popularity in European and North American countries, except for Britain.

The French Lop is a massive breed, having the heaviest bone structure of the Lop breeds. They are never to be long and narrow, with a body ratio of 2-1, meaning half as wide as long. It is the most Noble Beast, yet the Teddy Bear of the rabbit world. Very muscular and large boned, the breed has a longer coat with roll back to enhance massiveness. Some strains develop trousers, bloomers or dust ruffles, which is loose skin along the bottom of the body. The ears hang close to the head in a horseshoe with openings inward and length usually 15-17 inches tip to tip. At maturity, ears should not exceed length of head by more than 1 ½ inches. Considered the closest thing to a dog in a rabbit, in appearance as well as personality, the French Lop has a ram or bulldog head and a somewhat long, broad tail.

Due to changing climatic conditions, many imported French were hard to breed, thereby causing some people to outcross with breeds like the Flemish Giant. Other outcrosses have been made and continue to be made by some breeders to develop new colors. French Lops may show control of ears if crossbred to a rabbit with normal ear carriage.

In 1975, body type was lost to emphasis on head and ears—a massive, full, round head with good ear and crown, which is bone and cartilage complemented by length of coat. Does have a more narrow head and muzzle than the bucks. The skull of the French continues to grow until 25 months of age and the body and fur until at least 18 months of age. Inexperienced breeders sometimes discard good stock at an early age of development. Raising French Lops is a most rewarding experience, but they are not a breed for the impatient.

French Lop

CHARACTERISTICS OF THE MODERN FRENCH LOP

Possessing delightful personalities, they are the most lovable and easy to handle regardless of their weight and size. Their growth stages are as follows: Around six weeks of age, they depict a miniature body type of adult French; then they enter the rangy, bone-making stages; then they start fleshing out. They mature at one year of age or later.

The French Lops thrive on human companionship, can be housebroken and live in harmony with other pets. It is easy to understand why the personable French Lop is a fascinating and very popular breed of rabbit and thought by many to be the "ideal pet." With regard to personality: one must be able to differentiate between meanness and playfulness, as they demand attention and are known to become jealous.

The French Lop is lackadaisically inclined and the Bloodhound of the rabbit world, and therefore is not only an excellent companion animal, but it is also successfully used in animal-assisted therapy programs throughout the United States. The French Lop is the Teddy Bear of the rabbit world and maintains a position comparable to that of the Rolls Royce in automobiles. Less demanding and quieter than a dog, the French Lop is becoming a household word and most favorite pet. In short, the French Lop is more enchanting than ever.

FRENCH LOP STANDARD

Both the American Rabbit Breeders Association (ARBA) and the British Rabbit Council (BRC) have published official standards delineating the ideal French Lop Rabbit; rabbits in show competition are judged according to the degree to which they fulfill the model defined by the standard. The standards of both national associations are subject to modification from time to time, and new standards are published as required. Full standards can be obtained from the associations involved.

There are two varieties of the French Lop: solid or self colors and broken colors (colors broken by white). The colors within each variety are not judged separately: all solid colors are grouped together and the various broken colors are considered a separate group.

General type is allowed 75 points. Body is given 40 of these points, head and ears each 15 points, and feet, legs and bone 5 points.

Fur is allowed 8 points, color and markings 12 points and condition 5 points, out of a possible 100-point total for the French Lop.

SHOW ROOM CLASSES AND WEIGHTS

Show room classes are not only divided into two separate color classes (broken and self or solid), but also divided by sex and age. Weight is taken into account when determining the proper class, regardless of age.

Bucks and does under 6 months of age and not over 10 pounds are Juniors. Does 6 to 8 months old and not over 12 pounds and bucks 6 to 8 months old and not over 11 pounds are Intermediate. Does 8 months old and older and not under 10 pounds and bucks 8 months old and older and not under 9 pounds are Seniors.

Mini Lop

HISTORY

The first Mini Lop was known as the Klein (Little) Widder (Hanging Ear) and seen in 1972 at the German National Rabbit Show held in Essen, Germany. There were only 46 in existence at that time in Germany and were a cross between the German Big Lop and the little Chinchilla rabbit, bred in two colors, agouti and white.

Bob Herschbach of Watsonville, California, shipped three Klein Widders, a pair of agouti and one white doe, to America to display at the American Rabbit Breeders Association Convention in Ventura, California. Two years later, the breed name was changed to Mini Lop and was accepted by the American Rabbit Breeders Association on January 17, 1981, with a chartered specialty club of over 500 members.

The Mini Lop is not just a small French Lop. The Mini Lop is the result of crossbreeding or mating of distinct pure breeds of rabbits, mainly the French Lop with the little Chinchilla and the Netherland Dwarf. Because of the variety of rabbit breeds used in developing the Mini Lop, there are many colors in the background. The broken color was bred in America using the French Lop. Because of crossbreeding, the Mini Lops have had a tendency to revert to their normal, erect-eared ancestors with size and malocclusion major problems.

CHARACTERISTICS OF THE MODERN MINI LOP

Because there is much inbreeding to produce the breed, much ruthless and relentless culling is required to eliminate undesirable genes. Litter after litter has been destroyed because of serious teeth, ear and size problems. Size is difficult to control without a lot of inbreeding, which may adversely affect stamina, health, disposition, development and the digestive system. The Mini Lop is indeed a challenge to conform to the man-made standards, 4.5 to 6.5 pounds. Raising too small a breed leads to kindling problems in passing heads that are too large.

Mini Lop does are consistent breeders all year 'round, rich milkers and excellent mothers, raising five to eight babies. They are overly protective of their young and can be very aggressive during mating to the point of injuring the buck. Because of their rich milk, it is recommended that hay be fed daily to prevent diarrhea in the kits.

Breeding Mini Lops that are short in loin will result in lesser weight and size. A short, broad head with a short muzzle indicates a short body. Size is a genetic trait and should not be the result of withholding food and thereby sacrificing mental and physical well-being to control growth.

Ears should drop down at six weeks of age. There should be no airplane ears or ears with a lot of control.

MINI LOP STANDARDS

Both the American Rabbit Breeders Association (ARBA) and the British Rabbit Council (BRC) have published official standards delineating the ideal Mini Lop Rabbit; rabbits in show competition are judged according to the degree to which they fulfill the model defined by the standard. The standards of both national associations are subject to modification from time to time, and new standards are published as required. Full standards can be obtained from the associations involved.

There are two varieties of the Mini Lop; solid or self colors and broken colors (colors broken by white). The colors within each variety are not judged separately: all solid colors are grouped together and the various broken colors are considered a separate group.

Mini Lop

General type is allowed 70 points. Body is given 40 of these points, head 10 points, ears 15 points and feet and legs 5 points.

Fur is allowed 10 points, color and markings 15 points and condition 5 points out of a possible 100-point total for the Mini Lop.

SHOW ROOM CLASSES AND WEIGHTS

Show room classes are not only divided into two separate color classes (broken and self or solid), but also divided by sex and age.

Bucks and does under 6 months of age are Juniors. Bucks and does 6 months old and older weighing 4.5 to 6.5 pounds are Seniors. There are no Intermediate classes.

A sample (reduced in size) pedigree used by the author.

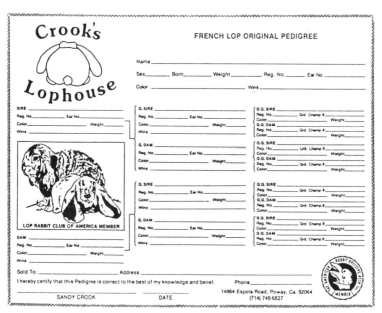

Holland Lop
(Netherland Dwarf Lop)

HISTORY

In 1964, an acceptable Dwarf Lop rabbit was created by Adriann Van de Cock of Tilburg, Holland, using small French Lops, Netherland Dwarfs, Dutch and English Lops.

In 1975, the Netherland Dwarf Lop was brought into the United States by Aleck Brooks III, founder of the Holland Lop Rabbit Specialty Club. He imported a pair of madagascar (tortoiseshell) and one sable point. It took Aleck Brooks five years to get the American Rabbit Breeders Association to accept the breed. Since the Association did not want a conflict with the terminology "Dwarf," the breed received a new name in the United States: Holland Lop.

In 1976, some American breeders were using the Netherland Dwarf and Dutch in their breeding programs to scale down the existing French Lop. Getting below six pounds to the desired three to four pounds was and still is quite a challenge. The pure Brooks/de Cock strain is the premium Holland Lop.

The Holland head is different from that of the French or Mini Lop. The head or skull of the Holland Lop is more "apple" shaped than that of the Mini Lop with shorter ears. Ear length from tip to tip should be 11—12 ¼ inches. The relatively light, short ears allows a degree of movement not seen in the French Lop. The "head" is the Holland Lop and decides the worth of the animal when judged at a show or for breeding. Ear carriage often leaves much to be desired as there is too much control of the ears.

Holland Lop

CHARACTERISTICS OF THE MODERN HOLLAND LOP

Good Holland stock is limited. The demand for quality far exceeds the availability. Prices of good de Cock lines can range in price from $1,000.00 to $1,500.00

The Holland Lop is tame, but widely found to be very mischievous, inquisitive, and timid. Holland does are doting mothers and good milkers, but very protective of new babies. Some have a very poor conception rate. Even though 8-10-week weaning is advisable, the does may not be tolerant of their litters for that length of time. Litters average two to four young, depending on the doe's size.

It has been found that human scent on nest boxes may pose a problem with breeder does who seem to prefer wooden boxes. Elimination of the problem is accomplished by using a butane torch for sanitation.

Being very hardy eaters, the Hollands have a tendency to overeat and get fat. On the other hand, starvation should not be used to achieve smallness. Dwarfism is a genetic trait. Starvation adversely affects the physical and mental health of any animal. It is a popular practice to breed large does to small bucks. Unfortunately, in an effort to keep the size down and stunt growth, some breeders practice and recommend breeding does as early as four months of age, even though one-half or more of the young are lost. Therefore, the purchase of senior animals is suggested to avoid any unpleasant surprises, especially with regard to weight.

Malocclusion and size in the Holland Lop lines are major problems. But a dedicated breeder who enjoys a big challenge will like breeding to perfect the Holland Lop, who does well outside and is very hardy. Strict culling is required to reduce size, establish type and correct teeth and ear problems. Though available in many attractive colors, there is much work to be done to fix the correct placement of color pattern in the broken color.

Holland Lop

HOLLAND LOP STANDARDS

Both the American Rabbit Breeders Association (ARBA) and the British Rabbit Council (BRC) have published official standards delineating the ideal Holland Lop Rabbit; rabbits in show competition are judged according to the degree to which they fulfill the model defined by the standard. The standards of both national associations are subject to modification from time to time, and new standards are published as required. Full standards can be obtained from the associations involved.

There are two varieties of the Holland Lop; solid or self colors and broken colors (colors broken by white). The colors within each variety are not judged separately: all solid colors are grouped together and the various broken colors are considered a separate group.

General type is allowed 60 points. Body is given 25 of these points, head 10 points, ears 20 points and feet and legs 5 points.

Fur is allowed 15 points, color and markings 15 points and condition 10 points out of a possible 100-point total for the Holland Lop.

SHOW ROOM CLASSES AND WEIGHTS

Show room classes are not only divided into two separate color classes (broken and self or solid), but also divided by sex and age.

Bucks and does under 6 months of age are Juniors. Bucks and does 6 months old and older with a maximum weight of 4 pounds are Seniors. There are no intermediate classes.

Selecting Your Lop(s)

Regardless of your reasons for purchasing your Lop, whether for pet or show or both, it is advisable to buy from a reputable, private breeder whose rabbitry exhibits good sanitation practices and good health and care. Should you decide to become a breeder, selecting the best will avoid much culling. Many Lops sold from unsanitary rabbitries carry with them latent or visible health and genetic problems. Every breeder knows the worth of his animals, which is reflected in management and price. Normally, rabbit mills, like puppy mills, sell bunnies cheap, much younger than seven weeks of age, without pedigree papers or tattoos, without really knowing the sex, without proper instructions on the care, and without transition food.

Lopping ears do not make an English, French, Mini or Holland Lop; pedigree papers showing three generations and an I.D. tattoo in the left ear of the Lop do.

People who consider price only fall prey to those selling lop-eared rabbits that are sickly, genetically defective and half meat rabbit with fraudulent papers. Unfortunately, they lose everything in the long run if looking for "a deal." Reputable breeders cannot help these people with their problems when it is not known for sure if they have a purebred Lop to begin with! Therefore, the following are guidelines for selecting your Lop(s):

1. Contact an established, reputable, active breeder who is a member of the American Rabbit Breeders Association, national and local specialty clubs.
2. Visit the rabbitry, which should exhibit good management through cleanliness, large spacious cages, and healthy, contented animals.
3. A quarantine section downwind and separate from the breeding stock for show animals and new animals brought into the rabbitry should be obvious. Though some breeders claim to never need to resort to such

measures, or do so only haphazardly, without fail, there are health problems (usually pasteurellosis) present in the rabbitry.

4. There should be a special isolation area for sick animals.

5. In the same light, rabbitries that stud out or have stud services available to the public should keep the community buck for this purpose in quarantine indefinitely and not use him in the rabbitry.

6. View the parents or sire and dam of the offspring in question.

7. Other breeds housed specifically for nurse or milk does to raise young Lops is an indication of poor reproduction qualities and poor foundation stock.

8. The breeder should show you stock with straight legs, good teeth or proper occlusion, clean ears, genital area for proper sexing and cleanliness, pedigree papers (even when not purchased), a correlating tattoo in the left ear, and clean nostrils. Breathing should be easy and noiseless and does should be checked for mastitis. No unusual lumps beneath the skin should be felt or be obvious on the body.

9. Pedigree papers should be complete and signed by the breeder. Imported stock on pedigrees should show at least a ring or ear number. (In some countries a ring is placed on a rabbit's hind foot as a form of identification. Rings are required to show in England.)

10. If looking for a prospective show animal, the breeder should stack the Lop in a proper show pose and evaluate overall balance, checking shoulders, rib spread, fullness of loin, fullness of hips, square hocks, toenails and tail. Between four to eight weeks of age, correct type for French, Mini and Holland Lops appears as a ball for the head with a larger ball

for the body. This is followed by awkward, growing stages, but correct type and balance appear again at maturity. Flat shoulders in a young Lop is one fault that will never change, but most other faults seem to correct themselves with age. The English Lop body profile should be mandolin shaped. Disqualifying faults are snuffles or respiratory disease, tumor, rupture, blindness, obviously torn ears, off-colored eyes, wall eyes, moon eyes, unmatched eyes, spots or specks in iris, malocclusion or broken or missing teeth, crooked feet or legs, bowed legs, severe cow hocks, deformed bones, foreign colored spots in solid varieties, wry tail (permanently set to either side), screw tail, bob tail, broken tail, bucks not showing both testicles in normal condition, white toe nails to disqualify in solid colors, colored toe nails in white or white-marked Lops, and absence of toenail or nails, including dewclaw nails.

11. Lops should not be adopted younger than seven weeks of age because undue stress is very detrimental to the Lop's physical and mental well-being.

12. The breeder should give transition food if the purchaser does not have the same brand of rabbit pellet fed the Lop at time of purchase.

13. Proper handling and grooming procedures such as cutting nails and cleaning ears should be demonstrated by the breeder to the purchaser.

14. Look for compatible disposition. A nervous or excitable Lop will cause numerous problems, not only as a pet but also as a breeder, which may result in sore hocks, poor maternal instincts and susceptibility to disease because of a low tolerance of stress.

Using the above guidelines, you will find a pet that brings company to the lonely, joy to the sorrowful, levity to the serious, love to the unloved—an investment in the future whose return will be threefold—the Lop!

Handling

There is much to be said about the proper way of handling and holding your Lop. Lifting by the ears is very harmful to any rabbit and should never be done. Very small Lops can easily be lifted by grasping the nape of the neck and shoulder area with one hand while supporting the hindquarters with the other hand. If the Lop is taken from a cage, turn it around and take it out backwards to avoid catching its feet and breaking toes in the wire. Big Lops are easily grasped at the shoulder with one hand while supporting the weight under the hindquarters with the other hand. Lifting large Lops from the base of the neck tears tissue and capillaries in this very sensitive area. The shoulders offer natural protective padding and resiliency when used as handles.

I encourage new Lop owners to practice lifting their new Lop from a table in the rabbitry before leaving with their pet. Always stop a runaway Lop from the front and never the back to avoid giving him a feeling of being caught in a snare or trap. Use of your chest for security and support is imperative to give the Lop a feeling of stability. The Lop's skeletal structure is smaller than that of a cat in proportion to his weight and he cannot right himself like a cat when dropped. Therefore, until a feeling of trust is established, because of fright, the Lop will kick and scratch when mishandled. You can see a sign of fear when the inner, or third, eyelid shows or appears in the inner corner of the eyes. When this happens, great pains should be taken to reassure the Lop of his safety in your hands.

For a right-handed person, I suggest bending over the Lop and quickly reaching under his body with the right hand, placing the first finger between the front legs. Simultaneously, reach around under the animal with the left hand to in front of the hind legs and cup the rump in your palm with your wrist across his hind legs. Lift the Lop to the right of your chest using your chest and upper right arm for support. In this position, a Lop is very secure and cannot scratch with the hind legs because of his being held firmly against your body by your left wrist. When the Lop seems calm, you can drop your left elbow and pull your left wrist from in front of the legs to under the feet, thereby supporting the feet and rump with your wrist and hand. Never grab and hold both feet together as this terrifies a Lop who thinks he is caught in a trap.

The nervous Lop can be naturally tranquilized by slipping his back across your chest to your left arm and repositioning your left hand to support the rump. Make sure his head lays back and he is flat on his back. Should his head come up or turn to the side, he will become frightened of his insecurity.

A Lop is a great companion for the horror movies on TV and will be very content through it all lying on his back between your thighs. Make sure you bend over your thighs while holding your Lop against your upper body and lower him until his back meets your thighs. This eliminates the feeling of falling away from you and reassures him in this new position. Do not trust a young Lop to stay content at first. Keep him wedged comfortably between your thighs with his head towards your knees and stroke his head between his eyes. Be ready should he startle from a loud noise or a sudden realization that he is in a vulnerable position. When you lift him up, bend down to him to do so.

The initial, secure handling is a major step in the right direction for truly enjoying and bonding to your Lop. When the trust becomes apparent, handling will be very easy and then you can show off to your friends your live stuffed toy.

Lops love affection. Petting should be done about the upper half of the body. They love to have their heads petted and kissed. Be careful not to continuously pet a developing crown on a young Holland, Mini or French Lop as this may flatten the muscle and cartilage at the base of the ears. Also, the stomach is a very vulnerable point for the Lop and only a very trusting pet will enjoy this type of caress. The Lop's weapons are his hind feet that are used to disembowel his enemy.

If your hold on your Lop is lost unexpectedly, sink to your knees quickly to lessen the fall. Lops have been known to break their necks, hips, backs, and legs from mishandling and falls.

This is not to say that the Lop is as fragile as a piece of china and therefore to be handled only rarely. In truth, being an active member of a family and the recipient of many signs of affection is the most important part of a Lop's life. So go ahead and handle him, now that you know how. The Lop will not be harmed by being held and loved, but can, in fact, die of a broken heart if left unattended in even the safest spot.

Housing

OUTDOORS

Proper sanitation, good ventilation, shade and protection from inclement weather and predators are the needs to be met with regard to housing the Lops.

When possible, galvanized wire cages are recommended. Floor wire is ½ inch by 1 inch, 16 gauge smooth galvanized wire, which is comfortable for the feet, with the ½ inch wire up or against the feet. The 1-inch or reverse side of the floor wire is rougher on the Lops and can cause sore hocks. Do not use hardware cloth, which is ½ inch by ½ inch because it does not allow droppings to fall through; also it sags and can cause an adverse chemical reaction to urine resulting in a swollen, infected genital area.

Chicken wire should never be used as it is flimsy, rusts easily, offers no strength to keep Lops in or predators out and has sharp twisted wire ends that poke and puncture and cause abscesses. Top and side wire should be strong and safe galvanized 1 inch by 2 inch, 14 gauge. Breeder doe cages used for kindling should be larger than those allowed for a single Lop and have ½ inch by 1 inch babysaver wire 4 inches high from the floor along the sides. Wire is manufactured with the baby saver feature. If not available, a strip of ½ inch by 1 inch wire attached to the 1 inch by 2 inch wire will do, though it collects debris. One inch by 1 inch wire should never be used, as teeth are often caught in this size wire and pulled out. If partitions are used, make them with ½ inch by 1 inch wire, two panels, 2 inches apart. This eliminates bitten ears, noses and feet, and helps prevent the spread of disease which is usually done through nose-to-nose contact. Cages should be free of sharp or abrasive surfaces and supported in such a manner that they can be easily cleaned. Trussed floor supports made of heavy galvanized steel can prevent floor sag if installed solid side underneath and against cage floor front to back. Doors and

Housing

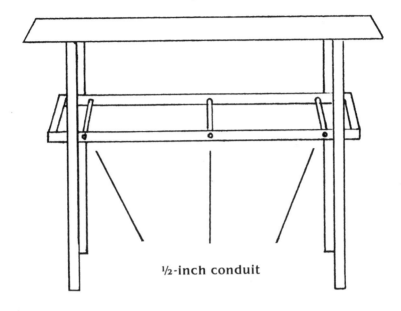

Roofed wooden frame designed to hold cages securely but still allow their easy removal from the frame.

openings should be large with doors opening *out* and to the side with good latches and framed with heavy No. 9 wire. Doors opening inward will continuously hit the Lop in the face causing aggressiveness and resentment. Special moulded plastic door guards can be obtained and snapped in place along door openings, thus eliminating sharp wire edges.

Cage assembly is done with cage clips ("J" clips) made of galvanized steel, 3/16 inch by ½ inch for clipping together two wires, and 3/8 inch by 5/8 inch for clipping together three wires. Use specially designed clip pliers and to remove clips use a specially designed cage clip remover tool.

Housing

It has been stated by some rabbit authorities that rabbits do not need much room and do not utilize extra space given them. This conclusion was drawn from observation of many rabbits in a large cage huddled together in one area, especially on hot days. What has been overlooked is that rabbits are animals of stress and when stressed because of crowding and/or heat, will huddle together for safety or relief. Therefore, what is observed is a stress reaction and nothing more. Stress may bring about enteritis and other health problems.

Cage size is dependent on the size of the breed and whether or not it is used for kindling (giving birth to young Lops). It is imperative that the cage allow a feeling of spaciousness for the Lop, especially for a doe and her babies or kits. Cramped quarters can lead to a shorter life span, depression, going off feed or starvation, illness, wire pulling, aggressiveness, refusing to care for young, turning on young, fighting, and enteritis.

English Lops and French Lops will do well in cages 4 feet wide by 30 inches deep by 18 inches high. When possible, stud buck cages 24 inches high allow more head room for both the Lop buck and the breeder. Kindling cages should be 6 feet wide with babysaver wire. If available, 24 inch high wire with the babysaver feature is excellent as this allows the doe room to perch on top her nest box, which is her sanctuary from her kits. Door openings should be large, not only to accommodate the Lop, but also the large nest box. Recommended door openings should be 17 inches wide and 13 inches high with doors opening out and to the side. A properly positioned nest box will prevent the door from opening inward.

Solid wooden floors have an 8 inch strip of ½ inch by 1 inch galvanized floor wire along the back of the cage to facilitate cleaning. Solid wooden floors are more comfortable, lessen stress and keep good weight on the hindquarters, but without meticulous management can lead to sanitation and health problems.

Housing

Mini Lops vary in size and do well in cages 3 feet wide by 30 inches deep by 18 inches high. Kindling cages should be 5 feet wide with babysaver wire. Door openings should be large enough to accommodate the Lop, nest boxes and breeder and therefore should be approximately 14 inches wide and 12 inches high.

Holland Lops do well in cages 2 feet wide by 30 inches deep by 18 inches high. Kindling cages should be 3 feet wide with babysaver wire. Door openings should be approximately 14 inches wide and 12 inches high to accommodate the nest boxes and breeder.

Security is important not only in keeping the Lops contained and unable to escape, but also in keeping out intruders and predators. Therefore, I recommend building a wooden frame with roof and legs independent of the wire cage, thereby allowing the cage to slip in the frame, or be removed or lifted for easy cleaning. Use 4 inch by 4 inch lumber for the legs and 2 inch by 4 inch lumber for the horizontal frame, with holes drilled through the center of the 2 × 4's on the 4 inch sides, to support ½ inch conduit upon which the cage will rest. The cage is slipped into the framework and is securely held in place, as the cage is recessed when dropped onto the conduit supports. This eliminates dirty, hard-to-clean corners and renders the cage itself portable. The roof should be slanted and made of ½ inch plywood and covered with waterproofed, light colored roofing. The roof should slope to the back for water runoff. and extend about 12 inches beyond the framework on all sides. For more security, the legs can be sunk in the ground at least a foot with the buried wood protected against rot with creosote.

It is best to have the cage at adult waist level to discourage harassment by dogs or other predators. For maximum security, I strongly recommend placing padlocks on hutch doors whenever possible to discourage pranksters and serve as a checkmate for malfunctioning cage latches.

Housing

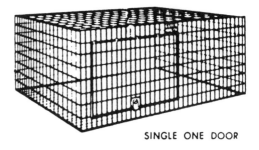

SINGLE ONE DOOR

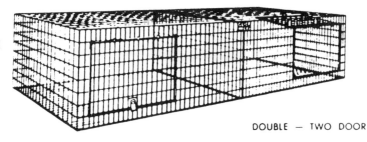

DOUBLE — TWO DOOR

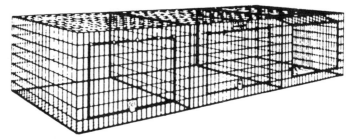

TRIPLE — THREE DOOR

The cages shown here were designed for use with commercially raised meat rabbits and are definitely unsuited for use with Lops.

Cages at waist level also make daily management much easier and more pleasant.

If possible, build the hutch under a tree to take advantage of the shade in the summer. The hutch is best with its backside against the prevailing wind direction, and facing in such a way as to allow a spacious view to the outside, in a quiet area. Waterproof, cloth tarpaulins hung from the top of the hutch attached just underneath the roof overhang at the top of the frame, make excellent portable walls, which can be dropped for shade, or protection from drafts, or rain during inclement weather. Normally, the tarps are hung doubled under, half-long, giving shade and allowing good air circulation. Folding tarps under keeps rain, leaves and dirt from collecting in and weighting and rotting the tarps.

Lops housed outdoors must be in well-ventilated areas away from excessive drafts, dampness, humidity, direct sunlight, temperature extremes and excessive, loud noises. Outdoor individual hutches offer the ideal situation, weather permitting. Open air circulation is of significant importance in a healthy rabbitry.

As an alternative to individual hutches, all cages can be hung under *one* roof, again of a light-colored material to reflect the sun, using wood, bamboo, shade cloth, tarpaulins, or similar materials for walls. It is desirable that the walls of the enclosure not only afford protection from inclement weather, but also the much needed ventilation in summer and winter. If buildings are used, they may have wooden walls, where the lower halves fold out and upward and hook in place to allow open air ventilation. The openings are best covered with wire to keep out predators. The panels are dropped back down in the winter. Also, buildings may have sliding walls or huge doors for ventilation purposes. Lime can be used on the ground to help control moisture and eliminate fly breeding sites.

It is imperative that there be a minimum of 20 total air changes per hour throughout the entire rabbit building. Improper ventilation guarantees sickness and death. A building should have vents and fans to circulate the air continuously, especially during closed-in winter months. In climates with below-freezing temperatures, a building should be heated to keep the water from freezing. A minimum ammonia level in a rabbitry is of paramount importance. High ammonia levels inhibit the action of cilia in the rabbit's trachea, thereby exposing the lungs to all the bacteria, microfungi and dust in the atmosphere. Clean, fresh air through good ventilation assists the natural defense mechanism leading to healthier stock. Do not reduce ventilation to maintain temperature in winter as it increases the humidity level, which then promotes disease. Solar heating systems have proven successful and economical in heating rabbitries.

INDOORS

If the Lop is to be kept indoors, an indoor Lop training cage is the best training aid. An indoor training cage comes in four sizes: 24 inches by 30 inches by 18 inches (recommended for the Mini Lop or Holland Lop), 36 inches by 30 inches by 18 inches high (recommended for the English and French Lops), 24 inches by 30 inches by 24 inches high (recommended for more head room for possibly a pair of small Lops) and 36 inches by 30 inches by 24 inches (recommended for more head room for possibly a pair of large Lops). The cage sits on short legs and a tray beneath is held above the floor or carpet and is easily removed for cleaning. The whole cage is made of galvanized steel and wire and has urine guards or deflectors four inches high around the cage floor, except at the door. There is a floor support and a large door 14 inches by 18 inches high, framed in heavy No. 9 wire, that opens out so the Lop can enter and exit at will. Too small a cage can become a prison rather than a training aid and haven.

Lops can be kenneled in a larger area using 1 inch by 2 inch galvanized wire on a sheltered, well-protected patio adjacent to a house with use of a litter box.

Housing

ACCESSORIES

Commercial metal rabbit ("J") feeders do not allow a bulldog-faced Lop enough head room. I have seen a French Lop become so frustrated with this type of feeder that he lost weight, developed poorly and eventually starved to death. Lops eat and drink out of stoneware crocks, much like dogs and cats. The # 1 small crock (4 inches in diameter and 3 inches high) which has a 16 ounce capacity is recommended for feeding small Lops, including very young English and French Lops. The # 2 medium crock (6 inches in diameter and 3 ½ inches high) which has a 32 ounce capacity is recommended for food for the large Lops and for water for the small Lops. The # 3 large crock (7 inches in diameter and 3¾ inches high) which has a 48 ounce capacity, is recommended for water for the large Lops. There are larger crocks available which can be useful for water for a number of Lops. Wash crocks thoroughly monthly or oftener, using soap to clean and chlorine bleach and water to disinfect. If there is no disease or health problem involved, crocks can be sufficiently cleaned in a dishwasher using hot water.

Large 32 ounce plastic bottle waterers are recommended for backup when more water is needed, i.e., a doe and litter, and as assurance of a water supply for the sporting Lop who likes to "bowl" with the crock or play in the water. Automatic watering systems are not recommended as they do not give an indication of a Lop off water, can spread disease, prohibit individual treatment by water medication, vitamins, etc., do not supply a Lop with a cooling system (hanging the ear in or standing in the water crock) on hot days, can (unknown to the caretaker) break down, and eliminate the personal attendance so very much needed to maintain a healthy, happy Lop.

Wire crock holders which hook onto cages keep crocks secure and in place for feed and water. These are especially useful in the indoor training cage, as they prevent the bowls

Housing

from bouncing around and overturning. Also very useful are holders for the #1 crock for each baby, plus mother, in a kindling cage.

A salt spool should be available and is best hung from the cage and away from the wire, using a salt spool holder made of rustproof aluminum or a nonrusting wire. Also, the salt spool can be secured to a piece of wood and then attached to the cage. Do not place the salt spool on the floor of the cage as it will coat the wire and lead to sore hocks and rusting wire.

A good grade plywood (CDX) sitting board is a must to relieve wire pressure, protect the Lop's underside from drafts and predators, and be used as a tension release for teeth and nails. This must be large enough for the Lop or Lops to lie down on and just small enough to fit through the large cage door to be placed in the center of the cage.

Last but not least, do not forget to provide a toy—an empty beverage can taped closed with stones inside and/or a metal canning ring.

SANITATION

Daily cleaning of hutches is of major importance in the prevention of health problems. Brush the bottom wire of cages daily to remove fecal buildup. Brushes should be rinsed well with water, dipped in a bleach and water solution and hung to dry. I have several brushes to cover a day's use on separate cages and keep the bleach and water solution in a covered, one-half gallon pickle crock. The solution is one-third chlorine bleach to two-thirds water and is replaced periodically, as it loses its disinfecting properties with use and age. It is important to rinse the solution from galvanized wire and wooden nest boxes with clear water. Larger brushes are kept for use in disinfecting the sitting boards, entire cages, carrier cages and nest boxes with a 1-to-10 bleach/water solution.

Puddin' on leash with a cat's figure-eight harness.

Casey leaving his indoor training cage, ready to play!

Diet

A Lop will drink and not eat, but will not eat without drinking.

Feed should look good and smell good and not be buggy or contaminated in any way.

Rabbit pellets may look alike, but brands differ in contents and taste. Lower-priced rabbit pellets lack quality control and may produce toxins in the intestines resulting in enteritis and/or death.

A high-quality, high-protein (18%) commercial rabbit pellet is recommended for the Lops. The major ingredient in rabbit pellets is alfalfa meal, with suncured alfalfa meal not only the best for performance but also preferred by rabbits. A pellet with milo filler in its makeup is a primary cause of abortion. Do not buy or store pellets or any grains, seeds or hay in plastic bags, as plastic suffocates and sweats and leads to deterioration of feed, which in turn can lead to enteritis, the second biggest killer of rabbits.

Rabbit pellets are available in 25, 50, 80 and 100 pound bags at feed stores. Do not stockpile feed as it decreases in quality with age. Three months is the limit. Some feed stores may sell pellets from a bin in smaller quantities to accommodate single pet Lop owners. Pellets should be stored in metal garbage cans off the ground on pallets or skids, keeping them free of moisture, mold and vermin which can transmit bacterial diseases such as coccidiosis and parasites like tapeworm. Plastic garbage cans often emit a strong odor which may permeate the feed.

(Top, left): The third or inner eyelid is visible on this frightened doe. (Top, right): Before purchasing a Lop, check for proper occlusion. (Bottom, left and right): The author demonstrates the proper way to lift a Lop.

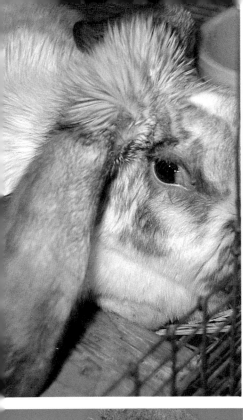

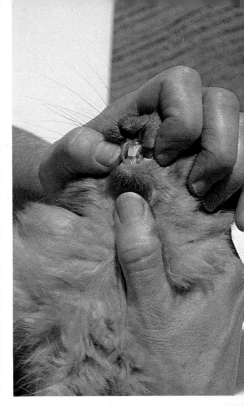

Diet

Hay is an important part of the diet and can be fed daily or several times a week as its effects add considerably to health, vigor and feed conversion. One handful placed on the sitting board will supply the needed roughage as a preventive to enteritis. The hay should be free of mold and poisonous plants such as milkweed, which is often found in first-cutting alfalfa hay. Milkweed has green, yellow broad leaves with fuzzy or woolly undersides, hollow stems containing a chalky substance, and is found in the Pacific Southwest.

It has been proven that growth is not hindered when a large percentage of the diet is good alfalfa hay. Good quality hay such as alfalfa or oat hay is a must not only to prevent intestinal blockages and/or enteritis, but also to keep a Lop eating during stress periods (after shipment, before and after kindling, inclement weather, diarrhea and sickness).

The Lop's digestive system is not designed to digest high levels of starch and other forms of readily-available carbohydrates. Grains, seeds and other additives containing a high percentage of grain should not make up more than one-quarter of the total daily diet in order to avoid a carbohydrate overload resulting in enteritis.

Hay should be stored in a dry place on pallets or skids, off the ground. Small amounts can be stored in paper or burlap bags, not plastic. Feed stores may give or sell smaller quantities of hay by the bag for single Lop owners who find a bale more than is needed, although lengthy storage does not affect the quality.

(Top, left): Two ounces is the daily ration of rabbit pellets for a Holland Lop. (Top, right): This fawn English Lop senior buck exhibits an excellent head and ear carriage. (Bottom): A senior French Lop doe with a senior Holland Lop buck demonstrate the largest and smallest of the Lop varieties.

Diet

Hay cubes are not a good substitute for feeding baled hay, as most qualities and benefits are lost through processing the cubes.

Food additives can be used to boost the nutritional value and energy level of the daily ration. Such additives should be fed in small amounts, from a teaspoonful to a heaping tablespoonful, depending not only on the size of the Lop but also its ability to digest rich foods. Introduce and increase the amount of additives slowly.

Lops will adjust the intake of feed to provide the needed energy level. As the energy level available in feed decreases, the amount eaten increases. Large- and medium-sized Lops can handle this, but the small Lops are limited because of their small stomachs. Therefore, the Holland Lop who eats about 2 ounces of pellets per day may starve to death or become malnourished on a low-energy feed, even if it is free choice, especially during the winter and during gestation and lactation.

Lops are people-oriented and sensitive creatures and should be fed and watered at the same time daily, preferably by the same person. Fresh pellets should be given daily in an amount sufficient to last the Lop over a 24-hour period. Pellets should not be left to stand for more than a 24-hour period as they pick up moisture unseen by the naked eye and spoil, which may force the Lop off feed.

The large Lops usually maintain themselves on 1½ cups of pellets daily. When hay is fed, less will be eaten. The amount of feed is commensurate with size, with the Hollands maintaining on approximately two ounces (¼ cup) of pellets daily. Remember to increase the amount of feed accordingly during winter, gestation, and lactation.

Crook's Punch, broken steel Grand Champion. (Below): A Holland Lop Siamese junior doe.

Diet

Dwarfism or size of Lop is a genetic trait and is not something controlled by feed. Starving is inhumane. You will sacrifice the Lop's mental and physical health to control growth.

Fresh water should be available at all times, given daily in a crock, thereby allowing the Lop to hang an ear in the water and lie next to it to reduce body temperature on a warm day (like a car radiator). Residue should be washed away daily from the crocks when they are refilled. Just adding water every day is asking for bacteria buildup and health problems. A small amount of chlorine bleach (1 teaspoonful per gallon) added to the water will keep bacteria minimal. Even though well water may be tested and found safe for humans, it still may cause problems for the Lops due to the bacteria present.

Water-soluble vitamins may be added to the drinking water to insure supplying the needed vitamins as feed loses valuable vitamins and minerals with age. I recommend using a pelleted additive with the normal pellet ration to avoid the possibility of increased bacterial buildup in the crock and the Lop refusing the treated water and not drinking the water which is so essential for its well-being.

It is mandatory that a plain (white) salt spool be hung in the cage—but not over the water or food crocks as it has a tendency to drip, due to condensation. Products other than a plain salt spool (e.g. mineral spools, etc.) are not recommended unless a specific diet deficiency has been diagnosed. Salt spools can be attached to a piece of wood and then secured to a side wall or hung by using a rust-proof salt spool hanger or wire. Though it is said by some that the feed itself has the required amount of salt, I have seen some Lops consume a salt spool within a short period of time. Just like people, some Lops need more salt than others, and who is to say that they would endure the hot summer months as well without available salt spools?

Following is a list of plants that should not be fed to rab-

Four does: Crook's Diana, showing large dewlap, is a Senior French Lop Broken Madagascar; the Senior English Lop is a tortoiseshell; at lower left is a Senior Mini Lop fawn; at lower right is a Junior Holland Lop frost point.

Diet

bits because most of them are poisonous while the others make poor rabbit feeds:

arrowgrass	bracken fern	broomweed
burdock	castor beans	poison hemlock
water hemlock	Johnson grass	laurel
mesquite	miner's lettuce	oleander
tarweed	buckeye	chinaberry
fireweed	foxglove	goldenrod
horehound	jimson weed	larkspur
lupine	milkweed	oak
poppy	sweet clover	

It is possible that even high-quality feed can go amiss; therefore attention should be given to the acceptance of and reaction of your Lop to a new lot of your regular brand of feed. Any change in the brand of pellets should be gradual. Obtain a small amount of pellets from the breeder when acquiring your Lop so you can make a gradual changeover to another brand if necessary.

Lops enjoy rolled barley, rolled oats, oat groats (which is the heart of the oat exclusive of the hull), sunflower seeds, rolled corn or corn on the cob in cold weather, carrots, celery, oranges, bananas, apples and fruit juices, to name a few. Corn is hard to digest and should be fed sparingly, and not to Lops under ten weeks of age. Only small amounts of lettuce should be fed, as it has a tendency to spoil quickly and may cause dreaded diarrhea or enteritis, the second biggest killer of rabbits. Fruit tree limbs with a few leaves (free of insecticides and dirt) are medicinal. Cabbage is not recommended because of its gaseousness.

Even though you will find your Lop will eat his largest meal in the evening, he will welcome an early breakfast treat and afternoon snack.

Mini Lop broken agouti senior buck exhibiting a narrow head and undesirable markings. (Below): Broken black Holland buck.

Diet

Rabbits have the unique ability to produce for consumption what is called night feces (a misnomer) which are soft, clustered, moist, small brown pellets full of protein, intestinally synthesized B vitamins and pantothenic acid. This not only aids in the efficient use of nutrients, but also sustains life in the wild when there is no food. The night feces are formed in the cecum rather than in the main intestinal tract and are eaten as they appear at the anus day or night. This is called coprophagy. It is a normal practice, not a sign of any deficiency, and maintains the normal intestinal microflora.

Rabbits will eat and cannot regurgitate bad feed; therefore it is important to exercise prudence with regard to your Lop's diet.

Crook's Patches, Grand Champion, shows the large dewlap present in does. (Below): This broken Madagascar Mini Lop buck is also a Grand Champion.

Grooming

Lops are very clean, but they need your help to look and feel their best. Routine checks from head to toe are a must. Ears and skin should be checked for crust, scabs and scale, a telltale sign of mites. If we were to have mites we could medicate and bathe them away, but a Lop with mites cannot reach behind its head and across its shoulders and back when grooming itself. Therefore the skin may appear red and the fur thin or missing, with scale and scabs obvious in this area when mites pose an annoying problem.

A good miticide—preferably one recommended by your veterinarian—will rid the Lop of mites. A cat flea powder will safely eliminate the skin mite problem. Usually, any medication used for cats can safely be used for Lops because they share the same skin sensitivity. Do not use a flea collar on a Lop as they do not accept anything around the neck. Pour the dust or powder in your hand and then apply it to the Lop in the affected areas, being careful that the Lop does not inhale too much dust. Repeat the following day and as often as needed until the irritation disappears and new fur growth is evident. I have heard of only one allergic reaction to treatment by a Lop, which resulted in sneezing and runny, watery eyes and nose.

Ears may show dirt, wax and/or crust. Using an eyedropper or other small applicator, place several drops of heavy mineral oil in the ear, filling the canal, and massage the outside of the ear canal in an upward and downward motion with thumb and index finger. The oil will smother any

A broken Chinchilla Mini Lop Senior doe in front and side views.

mites and bring to the surface any scale and wax not visible. Let the Lop shake his head, swab away the residue with wood stick cotton swab and repeat the procedure until no more matter is brought to the surface. Repeat treatment in six to ten days. I find using a four-ounce plastic bottle with a flip-top nozzle is useful in dispensing the mineral oil.

In extreme cases of ear mites, a miticide, possibly one that also removes wax, should be used. Because miticides do not kill mite eggs, treatment must be repeated in ten days. The Merck Veterinary Manual recommends swabbing the ears with one part Canex Solution (Oil Solution of Rotenone) mixed in three-four parts mineral or vegetable oil and applying the medication around the external ear and down the side of the head and neck. This is repeated after six to 10 days. Unfortunately, I searched a very long time for the Canex Solution only to find it available through a veterinary supply house in one gallon amounts at a costly figure. I found that treatment on a routine basis as a preventive measure caused undue irritation to the inner ear canal and in one case caused a serious skin reaction not only to the ear but also to the eyes. Needless to say, I dilute the Canex even more than recommended in all fairness to the more sensitive Lops.

If ears are left unattended, mites will irritate the lining of the ear causing serum and thick crusts to accumulate and cause secondary inner ear infections which can prove fatal. Hutches used by affected Lops should be cleaned and disinfected by using one part chlorine bleach to ten parts water and thoroughly rinsed with clean, clear water. Do not use strong products for cleaning areas or articles the Lop comes in contact with because the phenol present in these products is lethal to cats and rabbits.

Ear cleaning on a regular basis is a very important part of good grooming. (Below): The correct position for holding a Lop to check its teeth.

Grooming

Sometimes nothing is seen in the ear except the scratches caused by the Lop's attempt to rid himself of pests or some sort of irritant deep within the ear. And sometimes nothing at all is seen in the ears, but red and sore inner eye corners are evidence of an ear problem and are the result of constant ear scratching with the hind feet which invariably hit the eye area.

Unseen wax deep within the ear can build up and cause secondary infections. I use a nongreasy, nonoily cleaning solution for periodic, general cleaning. This type of cleaner is excellent to use before shows because it does not leave a greasy residue on ears and crown. These cleaning solutions may be procured through a veterinarian.

Always check the size of the ear canals to make sure they are not swollen and the passages are open.

For acute, secondary infections of the ear, a veterinarian can supply effective medication.

Unkempt ears can lead to numerous problems which may prove costly over a period of time. Be aware that an ear problem can occur when there was none at the time unnecessary treatment commenced.

Irritated eyes and inner corners of the eyes can be remedied by a terramycin eye ointment (ophthalmic). Weepy eyes may be caused by airborne dust, dirt or pollen and can be remedied by using a boric acid eye wash.

Check teeth periodically to make sure the occlusion has not changed through wire pulling, development, etc. To accomplish this, turn your Lop on his back, supporting his shoulders and spine with your hand and arm and supporting securely the haunches which are tucked under the same arm. This frees your other hand to pull away the upper or lower lip to expose the teeth which should appear as an overbite.

Lops make absolutely wonderful animal models!

82

Grooming

There are 28 teeth, with four upper and two lower incisors. The second pair of upper incisors is smaller than, and set behind, the first (peg teeth). If the occlusion is off and the lower teeth protrude past the upper teeth (undershot), clip the lower teeth close to the gum with small wire cutters. Clip the upper teeth if need be to correct the angle. Do not worry if the front teeth do not meet because they will grow quickly and the back teeth which are not visible will do most of the work until the front teeth are good again. If malocclusion is not attended too often, every two to three days, the teeth will grow into the flesh, penetrating the palate, deforming the gums and making it impossible for the Lop not only to eat but to live any length of time. A metal nail file should be used to eliminate sharp, jagged edges. Be very careful not to cut or injure the mouth in any way. When cutting, pull the lips away from the teeth, be careful to avoid the tongue and cut quickly, releasing quickly. Holding the cutters securely to the teeth for any length of time can result in a tooth being jerked out by the root and which may never grow back. The best position for this procedure is the same as recommended for cutting nails.

Nails should be checked and trimmed if necessary in order to help the Lop sit properly and to prevent total loss of a nail caught in a wire floor, broken toes, ear damage (especially the English Lops), or sore hocks from shifting weight to avoid discomfort. Use a small dog/cat nail trimmer to cut the nails. While in a sitting position, hold the Lop upright and against your chest like a baby. Lower the

Trimming a Lop's nails is important for grooming and health. (Below): The grooming tools you will need are available at most petshops since they are sold for dogs, cats and birds. There are a general comb and a flea comb, nail clippers, slicker brush and round-tipped bandage scissors.

Grooming

Lop to your thighs while still using your chest for security and place him on his back. Cradling the Lop between your thighs and closing your body angle to secure the hind feet, proceed to cut the nails up to the vein (usually where the nail initiates its turn downward) which will then recede from the end of the nail in time. In this position, the teeth can also be checked and sore hocks etc., treated without much fuss, since it places the Lop in a tranquil state. Talking in a low monotone helps maintain the Lop in this position.

Check the vent area and clean the scent gland crevices on either side with a cotton ball dampened with alcohol. Care must be taken to keep the alcohol from coming in contact with the genital openings. Usually a cheese-like substance and blackhead on the scent glands can be found and wiped away along with the odor.

If the vent area should need washing, hold the Lop over a bowl or bucket of warm water or at a faucet and wash it with castile, liquid organic or mild soap, rinse well and towel dry. Use a hand hair dryer on medium heat to quickly dry the fur to prevent chilling in cold weather.

Young Lops usually molt or shed at four to six weeks of age and have their first prime or adult coat at four to six months of age. Most Lops molt at least twice a year during a seasonal change starting from front to rear and from top to bottom. A small slicker grooming brush, metal comb and metal flea comb are excellent tools to eliminate fur knots and old, dead coat. The fine-toothed flea comb is not for fleas but for pulling out tufts of fur missed by the brush.

Check the area around the scent gland for cleanliness. If it requires cleaning, clean it as you would the genital area, using soft cotton wipes.

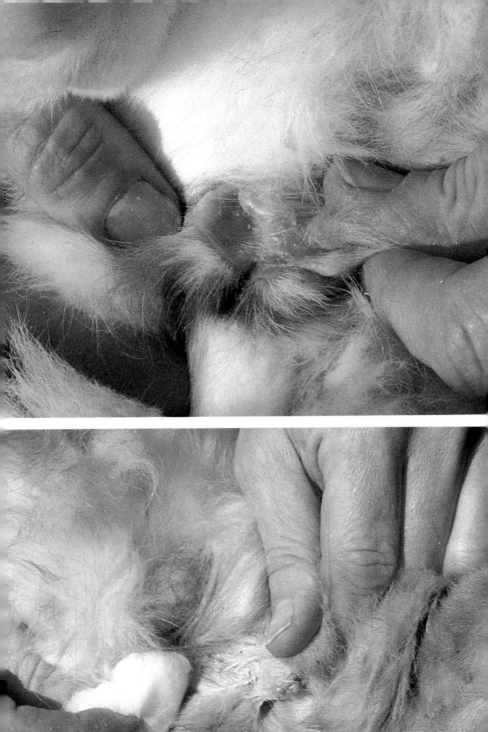

Grooming

Grooming your Lop during a molt will aid in preventing intestinal blockages due to fur balls. Continuous molting may be due to improper nutrition, parasites, heredity, etc. The complete molting process may take two to three months.

Fleas do not normally like the thick fur of the Lop and prefer hairy animals and humans. If the Lop is in good condition and exposed to fleas, you may find a couple on the ears where the fur is the thinnest. In that case, dust with a good cat flea powder.

My house Lop plays with four dogs and three cats. I dip my dogs, powder and flea collar my cats, and bomb my house every year. But in a year's time, I find only about four fleas and possibly none on my Lop.

Do not put a flea collar on a Lop. Rabbits' minds carry primitive instincts that will cause them to fight anything around their necks as they believe they are being snared.

Keeping your Lop in good condition is a constant job. Using your slicker brush (which is usually used for dogs), work out all the loose hairs area by area. This is especially essential during the molt. The lower photo shows what an agouti doe looks like in molt.

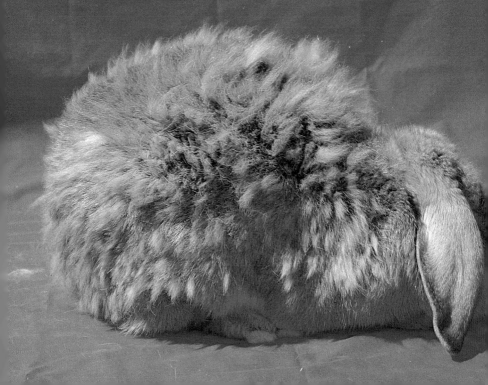

Housebreaking

Many Lops have been successfully housebroken. Some live indoors, while others are outdoor pets who have been litter-box trained, paper trained, pet-door trained or trained to nudge their keepers' legs to be let outside.

If you have not worked with a bunny before, it will be to your advantage to start out with a young one because of the size and ease of handling. Then again, older Lops appear to train more easily and have more tolerance in a new environment with amateur owners. The new environment should be as quiet and conducive to your new pet as to a new baby. In other words, no wild parties or loud music in his honor. Sometimes a Christmas Lop is best brought home after the seasonal excitement has quieted to a relaxed atmosphere, without constant holding and perhaps some molesting by the entire family. One family nearly lost a young Lop who was brought home to a roaring birthday party and was passed from person to person the entire day. That evening there was much concern when the Lop would not eat or drink and sat grinding his teeth in the corner of his cage. Fortunately this stressful situation was not fatal, but came close. Here, again, please remember to put yourself in your bunny's place and be considerate of his sensitive feelings as a stressing animal.

Confine the Lop to a small area with a litter box or other facility for toilet training. As outlined in the Indoor Housing Chapter, I recommend an indoor training cage specifically designed for the Lop rabbit. This cage has urine guards, a large door that can be left open for the Lop to enter or leave at will, and a bottom tray that can be easily

Two views of a very rare recessive color: a seal point Senior Holland doe.

Housebreaking

cleaned. There is also available a rabbit litter box 14 inches long by 24 inches wide and 3½ inches deep with a removable ½ inch by 1 inch galvanized floor wire with urine guards. This is cleaner than the use of a cat litter box, as the droppings and urine drop through the floor wire to paper or litter below.

If cat litter is used, make sure it is plain clay litter without any added chemicals like those little green granules that deodorize. These chemical granules are poisonous should the Lop decide to eat them.

I find old newspaper very satisfactory for use in the tray which should be changed daily to eliminate harmful ammonia fumes. A smaller baking pan can be inserted in a favorite corner of the big indoor cage tray thereby eliminating the need for gathering all papers daily for the Lop that uses only one small corner. Do not clean trays with strong disinfectants as the phenol contained in them is lethal to cats and rabbits as was the experience of a Lop owner who cleaned and rinsed the tray well every day, not knowing that unsuspected fumes would take the Lop's life in a matter of days.

It is unneccessary to disinfect a tray. If there is an odor buildup, the use of baking soda or an odor control product used for cats can be used in the papered tray.

I recommend placing the indoor training cage in a traffic area of the house. This helps the Lop to acclimate and relax as he can see what is happening around him and will want to be a part of the activity. Place your new pet in the cage and confine him until he urinates and defecates, preferably more than once. Allow him out of the cage or confined area or hold him for short periods of time (five minutes). When using an indoor training cage, make sure you turn the Lop

This three-week-old Holland buck is at an age when the ears begin to come down. (Below): A six-month-old broken tortoiseshell Holland Lop buck begins to show adult body type.

around and take him out backwards in order to avoid catching his feet and breaking toes in the wire. Place the Lop back in the cage or area to relieve himself. Should he go immediately, praise him for acceptable behavior and make a big fuss over him. You can let or take him out again. Lops love kisses about the ears. Avoid petting the developing crown on young Holland, Mini and French Lops. You may someday decide to show your pet and find yourself with a winner or Grand Champion. Who knows?

Toys are needed for the demonstrative Lop and a rattle made from a pop can with stones taped inside or a canning jar ring make excellent ones. A sitting board for inside the training cage will not only relieve wire pressure, but also serve as an outlet for nervous energy in the form of chewing and scratching. Also a small block of wood, small fruit tree limbs, or hay will help appease any gnawing tendencies and are cheaper than stringing electrical wire in your home through PVC pipe.

Gradually lengthen the time out of the training cage over the next several days. Remember, young Lops have a short concentration span, are constantly eating, have small stomachs and bladders and are very sensitive to change.

Some Lops are very shy at first and may take a couple of days to adjust. I find that a Lop willing to come out of his cage on his own is a sign of adjustment and an encouragement to continue training. Sometimes the owner sitting in front of an open cage while reading or the like raises enough curiosity in the most timid Lop to come out and investigate what it is that keeps you so busy. In other words, use the Lop's natural curiosity to your advantage.

(Top, left): A broken agouti French Lop senior doe. (Top, right): Constable's Bobby is a seven-month-old Holland Lop buck with two legs towards his Grand Championship. (Bottom): This fawn English Lop senior buck won Best of Breed.

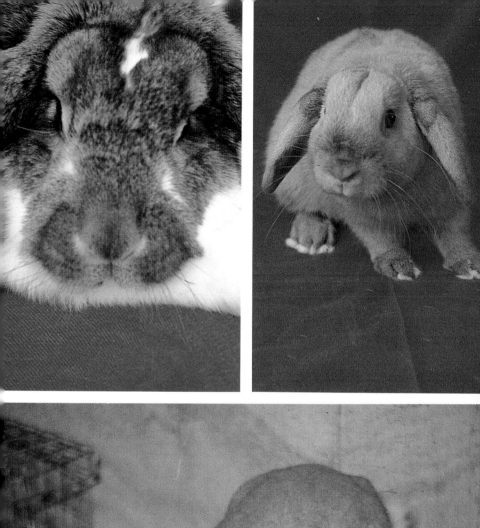

Housebreaking

Lops establish territory at about four weeks of age and experience stress when this territory is lost at weaning. It is therefore best not to unneccessarily relocate a Lop. For this reason, I do not housebreak Lops upon request because it is confusing and emotionally stressful to form a relationship and mutual bond to a Lop only to uproot him to be placed in a new home. The initial training should be done by the new owner.

It is advisable at first to play with your new Lop in a controlled space such as the immediate area where he is kept, or on a low table. Keep all movement easy and voices low and loving. Repeating the Lop's name with the word "come" and a treat will bring your pet hopping to attention. Use the same words repeatedly in training so that he knows what "no" is and what "good" is. If a mess is made, a firm verbal scolding and slight, firm shake before reconfinement is enough to make an impression. Reconfinement is the punishment, since the Lop loves his freedom. You may have to make a big impression by confining him for the day. Do not strike your Lop as you can dislocate his hip or back very easily. Hitting or tapping a Lop in the face is like a swordsman drawing his sword; in the rabbit world, this is a challenge and you can expect a duel! For this reason, doors that swing inward on cages often cause aggressiveness in a rabbit and doors that open outward should be used. As with any animal, teasing can bring about aggressive behavior. Do not throw anything at a Lop's face, not even his much-loved hay. In a couple of instances, an unsuspected acute inner ear infection was the cause of aggressive behavior; and then there was the case of the unsuspected pregnant doe thought to be a buck! Lops are individuals like people, so give yourself time to know and understand your pet and vice versa.

A magnificent portrait of a Grand Champion Mini Lop doe, Sandee's Gardenia.

Housebreaking

Should your Lop be placed on a table, make sure he does not fall. Sudden noise may frighten the most docile pet, which can lead to a broken back or leg. When of age and size, the larger Lops are capable of jumping onto chairs, beds and laps. Casey, my house Lop, was never placed on furniture and therefore does not jump on furniture. He does jump on my lap when I try to ignore the fact that he is around.

Do not allow your young Lop full run of the house. Just as children are trusted to play first in the yard and then on the block and then in the neighborhood, so it is with the Lop. Your house may not seem large to you, but from a young Lop's viewpoint it is overwhelming in size. Imagine its effect on the small, undeveloped mind connected to an uncontrolled bladder.

The Lop's housebreaking progress should be measured by the urine control and not the feces, which seem to just slip out like gas. With age, more control of those small marbles can be expected.

Lops occasionally test articles with their teeth, so be watchful with regard to electrical cords, furniture and plants. Catching your pet in the act of doing wrong is the secret to good training. Corrections can be made with a loud clap of the hands and shout of "no!" Sometimes reinforcement is needed by throwing a light, soft object near the culprit to demand attention. I recommend the "three-strikes-and-you're-out" method, which ends in reconfinement for a considerable period of time. Lops love their freedom and will soon learn that all is lost with unacceptable behavior.

Do not confuse ignorant disobedience with the purposeful disobedience that a rebellious Lop may exhibit to gain your attention and affection. Some Lops demand more of you than others, and that is a fact! Do remember that children are not expected to be perfect and child psychology comes into play when dealing with animals relative to their minds and behavior. I have witnessed erratic behavior in Lops to the point of death due to an emotional detachment and/or physical separation from the owner (human/animal bond). Be patient. Adolescence starts at three months of age and on the average, the Lop takes a year and a half to mature mentally and approximately two years to mature physically, especially in head development. There are times when you may believe you are feeding a program into a dead computer, but the day will come when all your good input will be played back to you by surprise and you will come to find living proof of the human/animal bond with your pet Lop.

There will come a time too when the cage door can be left open for the Lop to leave and return of his own accord for water, food, refuge and to relieve himself. You will find the Lop a basically shy pet around strangers—one who will seek refuge from a too busy environment.

An excellent example of a well-trained Lop is a housebroken doe whose home base or indoor training cage was in the kitchen. That is until one day when after the floor was washed, an oversight on the part of the owner left the kitchen bare. The mistress of the house could not understand the reason for her pet's getting underfoot and prodding. Upon returning to the kitchen, she realized her error and returned the cage to the kitchen corner. The doe, finding the door closed and no time to spare, jumped on top the cage and relieved herself through the top!

There are leaders and followers in any species and things are no different in the rabbit world. If by chance you find that your well-trained pet is regressing in its toilet habits, especially during adolescence, you may be looking at a leader or territorial Lop. Spraying and establishing new areas for urinating and dropping feces can be curtailed by castration of a buck or spaying of a doe by a veterinarian. Do make sure the veterinarian is familiar with rabbits under anesthesia since rabbits do not have much will to live and an overdose can prove fatal. A few Lops exhibiting such behavior have been known to outgrow these actions which may be due to age or season. It is best to have the Lop altered if you find your patience is wearing thin and your pet is becoming your pest. Once your Lop is neutered, you will find yourself with a less frustrated, lovable pet in a matter of days.

Please remember not to be too hard on your Lop should you find yourself with a territorial animal, as this is done by instinct because of hormones and no amount of punishment can stop a drive that is as frustrating to the Lop as it is to the owners. It is hard to accept a spray of urine across the legs from a happy, frolicking Lop as an act of love and possession, but such is the case!

Some Lops have been successfully trained to paper slipped under them at the appropriate time, especially the outdoor Lop when indoors. These Lops usually will seek the perimeter of a room and lift their tails slightly to relieve themselves, so you must be on your toes for this method.

Another method used for an outdoor Lop was to place a litter box inside the outside cage or hutch and then transfer the litter box to the house.

Whatever method you try to use in order to take advantage of the Lop's instinctive habit of "returning to the scene of the crime," remember—the important point is to make sure it initially happens where you want it!

The pet Lop will adjust to any lifestyle as long as he is loved and well cared for by his owners. A caged Lop will accept confinement only if it has been established and continued from day one. If freedom is part of his lifestyle, it cannot be taken away without its being a punishment. For instance, one of my therapy Lops, Cyrano, lived in a 4 foot cage in the rabbitry, happy and content. He knew when taken from his cage and placed in a carrier that he was either going to meet the public in a show, lecture, promotion or animal-assisted therapy. Cyrano loved the public attention while walking on a leash, running loose among a crowd or being held and loved by strangers. He accepted this lifestyle because he knew no other for comparison. When sold, he went to a pet home where he has all the fringe benefits 100 percent of the time instead of part of the time. I knew he could definitely handle his new lifestyle. Selling Cyrano to a breeder who had nothing more to offer than a cage for him to live in the rest of his life would have meant the self-destruction of this French Lop buck who would bound about his cage grunting with joy when he would see me coming for him.

Harnessbreaking And Tricks

Lops love to please and can be taught to walk on a leash, come when called, beg, jump through a hoop and play ball. Small rewards such as banana chips, thin wheat crackers, small pieces of banana and the like will do much to train your Lop.

For those of you who prefer to take your pet out on a leash and meet the public, a figure-eight cat harness works well as it can be easily adjusted to accommodate the growth of a young Lop. Three months has proven to be a good age to start placing the lightweight harness on him. To accomplish this, lay the Lop on his back in your lap and buckle up. Allow him to explore freely on the ground. Eventually he will come to the end of the leash and realize that you are in control. Start to take a few steps and give a couple of tugs, while calling his name and adding some audible kissing sounds for encouragement. If he does not respond or fights, soothe him and continue again when he is calm. An assistant, if available, should follow up with a slight bump on the rump if there is no response to the tugs. When he does take a few steps in the right direction, reward him verbally and physically even with a treat, making a big deal over his actions. Soon he will associate the tugs with the forward push and will come along on his own. Do not overdo it. Take your time—one step at a time. Do not stress him; this is supposed to be fun.

This brings to mind my first house Lop, PeeWee, who was trained to walk on a leash quite a distance to the mail box located on the main road. It was amazing to discover how out of shape the little guy was and therefore he was initially carried part of the way. It was like conditioning an endurance runner for the tortoise/hare race. Many times I was brought to realize why the tortoise always wins, and began to wonder, like my neighbors, about my sanity, as I spent so much time getting the mail for the sake of my "endurance runner."

Harnessbreaking And Tricks

The day came when PeeWee was programmed to go for the mail when the leash was snapped onto his harness. This was obvious to thousands of people during TV coverage showing the pet Lop hopping toward the camera with his friend Bunnye Meisel (true name) at the end of the leash. Suddenly PeeWee did a leaping about-face and took off like the White Rabbit in "Alice in Wonderland", with Bunnye explaining to the viewers, "He's going for the mail!"

The Lop can be trained to come if his name and the word "come" are spoken with treat in hand. This can be practiced while he is free or on leash.

Jumping through a small hoop or over a small bar or stick can be taught a Lop while in harness. Keeping the hoop or bar barely above ground, encourage the Lop with slight tugs on the leash to hop over the obstacle to a favorite treat in hand. With time, the obstacle can be raised little by little to a comfortable, maximum height. Again, training is slow but sure, and should be a fun, happy time for you and your pet.

The instinctive habit of "chinning," or placing scent on objects, makes the Lop a good candidate for pushing or nudging a ball back to you or an avid fellow ball player such as a Boston Terrier.

With time, encouragement and patience, you may find your Lop can be trained to do other tricks. But be realistic about his size when thinking about his fetching the paper or slippers. How about a pen?

Lops enjoy playing in water on warm days. Therefore, they can be taught to swim with you. Make sure your Lop can easily climb out of the water should he tire. If he needs to be taken out of the water by hand, be sure there is always someone present when he is in the pool, pool area or the like. Always make sure your Lop is dry before the temperature drops. Because wet fur is like wet cotton and takes a long time to dry, a portable, hand hair dryer may be needed to dry your pet to avoid pneumonia.

Showing

Showing your Lop at an American Rabbit Breeders sanctioned show can be fun and educational for a nominal fee. Your Lop will be judged in competition with other Lops of the same breed by a licensed ARBA judge, and the Judge's remarks about your Lop will be permanently recorded on a form and given back to you for your records. You will meet many other Lop fanciers who are more than happy to talk Lop with you. The breeder you purchase your Lop from will be able to tell you of clubs to join and shows to attend. Otherwise, contact the American Rabbit Breeders Association, Inc., Box 426, Bloomington, Illinois 61701, for helpful information.

PREPARING FOR THE SHOW

Groom your Lop well in advance of the show date in order to show him at his best. Last-minute discoveries have been the defeat of a possible winner. If your Lop's coat looks dry, the addition of sunflower seeds or wheat germ oil to the daily diet will help. If a coat is washed less than four weeks before a show, it will lack the natural oils necessary for a good sheen. Stains in white fur can be taken care of using hydrogen peroxide or vinegar and water (one-half vinegar and one-half water) followed by an application of corn starch. Brush out the corn starch when dry.

If the coat is badly stained from the urine of a spraying buck in an adjoining cage, it is best to place a solid wood partition up to block the spray and pray for a molt.

Make sure ears are clean. Do not clean them with mineral oil just before a show as the residue takes a couple of weeks to completely disappear. Make sure nails are trimmed and there are no lumps, bumps or sores to be seen. Your Lop should be the picture of health and vigor.

Showing

Look at the pedigree papers of your Lop to determine his age and then weigh him on a baby scale to make sure he is not over or under the weight allowed for the showroom classes. A judge will usually allow one-quarter of a pound over maximum weight in a class. If you find yourself with a fast-developing junior Lop, it is best to avoid putting him on a diet to make weight because many times you stress the animal's physical condition. Plan on showing him as a senior when he is of age, or show him anyway just for obtaining the judge's overall remarks about your Lop. You need not take the pedigree papers with you to a show, unless you plan on having your Lop registered by an ARBA Registrar, as the judge will check your Lop's left ear for the required tattoo.

TRANSPORTATION EQUIPMENT

Proper transportation equipment is essential when going to a show. There are show carriers or transport cages of various sizes to comfortably accommodate your Lop. These carriers are made out of galvanized wire and have carrying handles and metal trays. The largest carrier is 14 inches by 24 inches for a single big Lop. This size carrier allows the Lop room to stretch out with a carrot and room for a small crock of water or even one-half gallon milk carton or plastic liter frozen with water if needed. Remember not to add additional stress to an already stressful situation by packing your Lop in a small carrier or container like a cardboard or wooden box offering no ventilation.

If possible, transport your Lop during the coolest part of the day during the summer and make sure your Lop is out of direct sunlight, covering a window with some type of material to afford adequate shade. I transport my Lops in the back of a truck covered with a white fiberglass shell with front air scoops and large sliding screened windows on each side. If I leave on a cool morning of a very hot day, I take a cooler packed with containers of frozen water and a couple of gallons of fresh drinking water for the Lops. Otherwise, the containers are placed in each carrier and I attempt to drive nonstop.

Whether it be cold and wet or hot and humid, if the weather poses a threat to the Lop's health and well-being, do what I do—just don't go!

If you find yourself a veteran with many Lops to transport, you will find a Kennel Kart a worthwhile investment. I stack my carriers in pairs three high if need be, and secure them with bungie cords.

I find a laundry basket handy to tote my accessories: a gallon or two of water, a roll of paper toweling, tattoo kit and spray bottle of alcohol, pedigree papers and Records of Legs, a rug for placing on top of a carrier for grooming, a small spray bottle of water to help remove loose fur, a slicker brush, comb, cotton swabs, a pen, business cards and holders with clips to clip to the carriers, folding chair and lunch.

If the show is a fair, national show or convention where the Lops are cooped on exhibit for several days, I bring adequate feed, electrolytes or bleach (1 teaspoon per gallon of water) for the drinking water, and padlocks, which are allowed if they are removed during judging so that appointed qualified carriers can bring my Lops to the judging table.

ENTRY

Most local specialty club shows do not have pre-entry. You enter your Lop at the show before a designated time. Entry forms are obtained at the Show Secretary's table and are then filled out, denoting breed, self or broken, buck or doe, class and ear number and submitted to the Show Secretary with your entry fee. You are requested to write your name, address and number of Lops entered on a numerical exhibitors' sign-in sheet. This determines your entry number, which is then entered on your entry form.

Sit close enough to hear the classes called at the judging table. When your class is called, bring your Lop to the table and place him in a pigeonhole, usually designated by your entry form placed on the table. (That is why you must remember your entry number!)

SHOW RULES
Both the American Rabbit Breeders Association and the British Rabbit Council have instituted official show rules, and all exhibitors must abide by the rules of the national organization governing the showing of rabbits in their country. The rules current at any given time (the rules are subject to change, remember) are obtainable from the governing notional society. The following is based on ARBA rules.

*All entries must be owned by the exhibitor. Otherwise, the exhibitor is severely penalized.

*A Lop cannot be exhibited in more than one class in the same show, except for fur and pre-junior classes.

*Unsportsmanlike conduct is penalized by elimination of the exhibitor's entries and exclusion from the show. Such conduct may jeopardize the exhibitor's ARBA membership.

*Exhibitors are not allowed behind the judging table, unless authorized by an official or acting in an official position.

*Since only ARBA members can qualify to receive awards furnished by ARBA, membership is encourged and can be obtained through show officials prior to or during the show.

*The American Rabbit Breeders Association has Rules Governing Awards as specified in their STANDARD OF PERFECTION.

*Generally faults include moult, poor condition, stained fur, badly broken toe nails, foreign white hairs in colored fur, excessively large dewlap, poor tail carriage and eye color.

*Generally eliminations are temporary conditions and can be corrected, such as ear mites, obviously pregnant does, sores, dermatitis, abscesses, and illegible and misplaced tattoos.

*Generally disqualifications include Pasteurella (snuffles), tumor(s), blindness, severely torn or damaged ear(s), off-colored or mismatched eyes, spotted or speckled iris in eyes, malocclusion or missing teeth, crooked or deformed limbs or bones, foreign colored spots, deformed tail, monochrid, cryptorchid, missing toe nail(s), foreign-colored nails, and wrong sex.

*Exhibitors are not to interfere with the judging in any way or give any sign, word or indication to the judge which Lop belongs to whom. You are not allowed behind the judging table, unless authorized or bringing your Lop to or from the judging table. After your class is judged and your Lop is no longer in competition, you can feel free to ask the Judge a pertinent question. Most Judges welcome honest questions that do not interfere with the judging when asked at appropriate times.

*The American Rabbit Breeders Association has Rules Governing Awarding Grand Champion Certificates.

*A leg is a major win towards a Grand Champion Certificate and will be given to a Lop under the following conditions:

1. Wins first in a class of five or more entries owned by at least three exhibitors.

   Wins Best of Breed (BOB) or Best Variety (BOV) providing there are at least five Lops shown in the breed or variety by at least three exhibitors.

3. Wins Best Opposite Sex (BOS) or Best Opposite Sex of Variety (BOSOV) providing there are at least five of the same sex as the winner shown in the breed or variety by at least three exhibitors.

4. Wins Best in Show (BIS).

5. At least one leg must be obtained as an intermediate or a senior.

6. Legs are to be awarded by at least two different ARBA Judges at ARBA sanctioned shows. But two legs cannot be given at the same show for the same Lop.

7. Legs are to be obtained by the exhibitor from the Show Secretary either at the show or through the mail.

*A Grand Champion Certificate will be given to a registered Lop that has won at least three legs properly completed and endorsed and sent with a nominal fee to the ARBA Secretary. Only one Grand Champion Certificate will be awarded a Lop.

*Once a Grand Champion Certificate is obtained, in all fairness to upcoming Grand Champions and in the best interest of the stressing Lop, a Grand Champion should be retired and used to improve the breed.

*When judging is finished, a copy of your Entry Score Card (remark card) filled out by the clerk will be made available to you to take home. The card will not only show the Judge's remarks but also any reward received, the number of exhibitors, the number of Lops in the class, the sweepstakes points. (The Sweepstakes Point System is very misleading. Sweepstakes Points usually reflect number of Lops [quantity] and not necessarily the top winners [quality].)

AFTER THE SHOW

Unknowing or not, some people bring sick rabbits to shows. Therefore, I strongly recommend isolating your show animals from the rest of your herd for at least 30 days, feeding and caring for them last daily to prevent spreading germs and bacteria. Some breeders claim this is not necessary, but it is only a matter of time before such negligent practices catch up with their herd. The worst to be expected is pasteurella, the number one killer of rabbits. I recall a very good, successful breeder who brought back a renowned, winning, pregnant doe from a major national show, and failed to quarantine her. She had been exposed to pasteurella at the show and when she kindled, the outcome was tragic. The breeder was left to cope with multiple abscesses, much sickness and the death of approximately 80 Lops due to pasteurella. Years later, the breeder still dealt with problems in the herd because of this epidemic.

Clean out your show carrier tray, rinse it well with water and allow it to dry to keep the acid from eating the tray. Store your show carrier separate from any others to keep from spreading germs and bacteria. If needed for other uses, clean and disinfect the carrier with bleach and water (1 to 10 ratio), rinse it well with clear water and let it dry in the sun.

Regardless of your wins, without healthy Lops, you have nothing!

A sample entry score card.

Health

Years ago when I first became enchanted with the French Lop, I was appalled at the number of people, even those in prestigious positions, who had sickness and death as an everyday occurrence in their rabbitries. Today, many still accept and deal with it as a way of life, thereby setting the wrong precedent for newcomers to the world of rabbits. Why people accept this is beyond my reasoning—like the fallacy that pigs are stupid and filthy. The truth is, *it is the fault of the owners!*

With limited knowledge of the rabbit, even veterinarians have been known to treat and accept pasteurella or pasteurellosis as a common ailment, a common cold which all rabbits have, assuring the owners that it is nothing to worry about. The truth is that pasteurella is the number one killer of rabbits and is the reason why I have a quarantine section for incoming and show Lops. It is incurable in the majority of cases and highly contagious to other rabbits.

What I could not understand in the past is why all these problems exist and why they can't be eliminated. Much of the reason is that good rabbit management entails hours of one's time and leaves those who are less perfectionist to cutting corners to the point of being detrimental to the health of the rabbits. The soft, silent nature of the rabbit, especially the Lop, lends itself to much neglect which would not continue unnoticed had the rabbit been a vocal animal like a dog or cat. Instead, the rabbit stresses in silence at the expense not only of mental but of physical well-being. My heart goes out to the laboratory rabbit, a mute victim.

True animal lovers know that to do right by them is a labor of love. Good rabbit breeders know that the price of the Lop never covers the man-hours spent raising them. Usually the worth of a Lop goes along with the common law of business balance and is an indication of the quality of management, housing, diet and knowledge of the breeder. Breeders should not feel pressured by the many who, unfortunately, crossbreed to make quick money from the Lop. I guess there is hardly anything in this world that someone cannot make a little worse or sell a little cheaper, and for the sake of the Lop dedicated breeders should not succumb to the practice.

It is believed that 99% of the problems would not occur with proper management, which includes good sanitation. Among rabbit raisers there is too much indiscriminate use of drugs which is no more than a crutch in place of good management.

Feeding high-quality feed, taking time daily to manually flush and/or clean and fill water and feed crocks, providing adequate room, cleaning sitting boards and hangers (feces) from the wire, maintaining an effective rodent and pest control program, cutting nails, dusting fur mites, cleaning ears, checking teeth, cleaning nest boxes every two-three days, disinfecting when necessary, continuously providing protection from the elements (heat, cold, wind and rain), providing proper ventilation to eliminate ammonia fumes from urine, working with a veterinarian or the county or state laboratory for cultures and necropsies to understand and eliminate a problem, maintaining a strict quarantine and caring for problem or sick animals last results in a healthy, disease-resistant rabbitry offering healthy stock that will live on the average six to eight years and sometimes as long as ten and twelve years. Whether you are a 100-hole rabbitry or a one-hole pet Lop owner, the quality of your Lops is no better than the quality of management. However, it is very important that you start with healthy, hardy animals with an inherited resistance to a variety of bacterial diseases. Introduce Lops into the rabbitry from as few sources as possible in order to keep the number of strains of bacteria at a minimum and thereby avoid an overload and breakdown of resistance.

Health

The following information should be helpful to breeders with large numbers of Lops and as a reference to the pet owner to assist him in determining when to contact his Veterinarian and what he can do on his own in the event of a health problem or in an emergency. Additionally, this is to serve as a reference to veterinarians whose primary practice is not with rabbits. I must caution and advise you that I am not a veterinarian and that I highly recommend you seek the professional help and guidance of a veterinarian when in doubt and for major health problems. Considering the soft, silent nature of the Lop, I personally found it mandatory that the knowledge, treatment and procedures be taught and shown by a veterinarian and advise you do the same. The Lops are basically healthy animals; with good hygiene and preventive care and love, most of the following problems will never be encountered.

INTERNAL PROBLEMS

Symptoms of internal health problems are recurring soft feces, diarrhea, lack of normal amount of defecation, sneezing, nasal discharge, bloody urine, pinworms on the feces, continuous molting, scruffiness, loss of appetite, weight loss, abnormal behavior, abnormal movement, abnormal lumps or swelling and fever (normal temperature is 102°-103°).

Recurring soft feces or diarrhea can mean a nutritional problem such as too much of a rich food or one that the Lop is not used to eating, a carbohydrate overload caused by too much grain and/or seeds, a physical upset in hot weather, bad or spoiled feed, or contaminated water.

If any of these causes is suspected, take away the pellets and give only stalky alfalfa hay or the like (as leaves add richness) and add a ¼ teaspoon of chlorine bleach to 1 quart of water for drinking. Some water may have too high a bacterial count for rabbits even though fit for human consumption.

Wash the vent area, if need be, especially in the summer when flies can present a maggot infestation in a matter of hours. You should see a big improvement in 24 hours. If so, gradually add back the pellets to the diet, minus any additives, continuing with a handful of hay and bleach-treated water. Bleach must be added to fresh water daily as it dissipates in time.

If there is no improvement, a liquid antidiarrheal such as neomycin sulfate can be used together with straw and stalky hay and treated water. There should be an improvement within 48 hours. If there still is no improvement, it is recommended that all food and water be taken away for 24 hours. Then supply treated water and stalky hay.

If in doubt and symptoms persist, without delay, take your Lop to a veterinarian who is experienced in treating rabbits because diarrhea or enteritis is the second biggest killer of rabbits.

If in a bind, human remedies such as Pepto Bismol (½ teaspoon or ½ cc twice a day) may help until professional help is obtained.

My own personal experience with a bad lot of feed proved Neomycin Sulfate together with straw and hay to be the salvation of five of my French Lops. Assuming all recently-bought feed had to be good if it looked good, I fed a new bag of pellets that had a peculiar, almost rancid, odor to it. The following day, many of the Lops did not touch the feed. The few that did eat some were my most ravenous eaters. The diarrhea hit and the intestinal pain was so great that one doe bit a hole in her pop can toy. Many phone calls later, I found the cause was an unauthorized substitution of animal fat for a slicking agent by an employee. The animal fat turned rancid and caused a toxic reaction in the intestines of the Lops. Even though a test would prove the food not to be poisonous, ingestion by rabbits almost proved fatal. Needless to say, the feed lot was recalled and the error corrected.

I often wonder how many rabbits may have died from this feed before it was recalled while the owners thought that it was just another bug hitting the herd or wondering what they could have done wrong.

Kindling, nursing, hot weather and other stresses may produce a hormonal or physical upset causing a soft feces or mild diarrhea. Add electrolytes to the drinking water and hay to the diet. If no improvement, reduce the amount of additives given to an ample supply of pellets.

Coccidiosis may be the cause of soft feces, diarrhea, continuous molt, poor appetite, lethargy, rough coat, fur chewing, pot belly and death. An infected liver shows lesions. Coccidiosis is caused by a protozoan organism: one type infecting the intestinal tract while the other (hepatic) infects the liver (small white spots). Coccidiosis can be diagnosed by a veterinarian through a fecal flotation test. Lops that are allowed to play in dirt, kept in unsanitary conditions or brought to rabbit shows are good candidates for contracting coccidiosis.

Sulfaquinoxaline, sulfamethazine or other types of sulfa drugs are used for treatment. Lops that overcome coccidiosis may become carriers continuing to spread the disease, such as a doe to her young. The life cycle of the coccidia takes seven to ten days to complete at which time the oocysts (eggs) are flushed from the intestinal tract with the feces, causing soft feces or diarrhea which lasts for 12 to 24 hours. With the life cycle so short, a fecal sample should be tested for coccidia during this time. A fecal sample taken after a bout with diarrhea is usually negative; therefore, a sample should be obtained on a routine basis, like once a week. A daily stringent sanitation program is in order to control the disease since the spread of infection is through ingestion of contaminated feces. Keep areas dry. Most infections occur in very young Lops, even those in the nest box.

Commercial rabbit pellets containing sulfaquinoxaline (0.25%) will prevent the coccidia level from increasing, but will not rid the Lop of the disease. Many people believe that feeding these pellets will prevent the disease, but this is not true. Also, continuously subjecting Lops to a medicated feed will build an immunity to the drug over a period of time as resistant strains of coccidia will develop. Then what?!

Mucoid Enteritis affecting young rabbits is prevalent in most commercial rabbitries and the exact cause is unknown. It is thought to be related to digestive upsets, overeating, nervous tension and other stress factors. Treatment recommended is withholding solid food for 24 hours, then feeding stemmy alfalfa hay or similar roughage instead of pellets. Feeding pellets is resumed gradually upon improvement. Clinical signs are loss of appetite, dull eyes, possible gritting or grinding of teeth, rough coat, intense thirst, bloat (sloshing belly) and passing of jelly-like mucoid material from the bowels. Great pain is exhibited through sitting humped up, sometimes over the water crock and grinding of teeth. Temperature is subnormal. Death is primarily due to dehydration and occurs in 80 percent of the cases within 12 to 72 hours. Electrolytes such as Hydro-Lite or even Gatorade should be given to help prevent dehydration. Mild enemas, such as the disposable type, are helpful because of blockage of the colon due to diarrhea and mucous. When blocked, the gut stops working, the contents forms a gas, a bloated condition occurs, and the gut starts to rot. I believe mucoid enteritis is to some degree hereditary because affected Lops seem to be hyperactive or easily stressed.

Lack of normal amount of defecation usually goes hand in hand with loss of appetite, most commonly caused by an intestinal blockage. In severe cases, the Lop may bite his side because of pain and may lose normal use of a hind leg on the affected side due to the painful blockage and cramping.

Usually a recent molt is a contributing factor. Feeding a handful of hay several times a week or on a daily basis is recommended as it helps assimilate food and guarantees fiber needed to evacuate the intestines.

If a blockage is suspected, a cat hair-ball medication (2-3 inches) and hay should be used in large amounts until the Lop is back to a normal diet. Obtain the medication in a tube and feed directly into the mouth as much as will be consumed by the Lop who should be held in a reclining position. This will not cause diarrhea. In extreme cases, I have found that a natural herb laxative given in conjunction with the hair-ball medication eliminated the problem. I have never seen any unusual discharge resulting from using any of these medications. There are various hair-ball medications on the market available in pet shops.

Flavored heavy mineral oil, possible with mashed banana, may be given orally using a syringe. Unflavored mineral oil can easily flow into the lungs and cause pneumonia. I have found this to be very messy and it provokes much resistance. This is best administered by a veterinarian via a stomach tube. The veterinarian may find surgery necessary in severe cases.

Sneezing may be due to allergies to dust, fur, hay, pollen or fumes such as from paint, lacquer or even the galvanizing process used on wire. Check the nasal passages to see if there is a nasal discharge. Usually a milky discharge indicates the Lop is fighting something. It is wise to have the discharge cultured to determine if there is a disease problem. This should be done before administering medication as the medication may mask the problem and alter the outcome, unless there is a time lapse of seven to ten days from the last treatment.

Pasteurellosis, Pasteurella or Snuffles is one and the same biggest killer of rabbits, with common symptoms being white or yellow nasal discharge, sneezing, and matted inside front legs. Pasteurellosis can manifest itself in many ways, such as metritis (infection of the uterus), orchitis (infection of the testicles), mastitis (infection of the mammary glands), conjunctivitis (infection of the eye), sinusitis or snuffles (infection of the sinuses), inner ear infections, and subcutaneous abscesses. It is a very contagious bacterial disease in rabbits, and very few are cured. There is no such thing as a common cold in rabbits. More often than not, the problem is heavy growth of a bacteria known as Pasteurella Multocida which is normally in balance within the body of a rabbit.

When the balance is upset through extreme stress, poor management or excessive exposure to the disease, the bacteria runs rampant throughout the body. It grows like a cancer and is resistant to most antibiotics and may be eliminated only if caught in the very early stages. Oftentimes, Pasteurella is incurable once the disease takes hold, sometimes resulting in pneumonia and death within a 48-hour period. Drugs the bacteria is usually sensitive to are Chloromycetin, Cephalothin (Kefin), Gentamicin (Garosol), Kanamycin, Polymyxin B, Sulfa, and Tetracyclines (Aureomycin and Terramycin). After treatment, if symptoms reappear, it is wise to have the Lop put down, euthanized. Usually medications administered will curb the disease temporarily, but symptoms will reappear under stressful conditions such as transport or extreme weather changes.

New stock coming into the rabbitry or Lops coming back from shows should be placed in a quarantine section downwind and away from the rabbitry for 35 days. Unfortunately, sick animals are found on the show table. The risk of picking up Pasteurella, among other diseases, is very high. Rabbitries have been known to eliminate sickness when showing of their animals was eliminated.

With regard to disease, there are some animals that have the symptoms, some that are carriers without any symptoms, and those that are well. The ultimate test for a doe, even one thought cured of Pasteurella because of a negative culture, is kindling. Such was the case of a show doe who came down with an acute case of conjunctivitis just before kindling. Euthanasia was the only solution.

Bloody urine may mean cystitis (inflammation or infection of the bladder). The urine should be cultured by a veterinarian. Usually treatment is for one week with Chloramphenicol, Combiotic (pen-strep), tetracycline or sulfas. An infected doe should have her vagina examined for vaginitis as cystitis often follows vaginitis. Douche her with a mild iodine solution or nitrofurazone while treating systemically with an antibiotic. Do not breed an infected doe until you are sure the infection is gone, as vaginitis can be passed through the herd via the buck even though he does not get the disease.

Urine normally contains precipitates of inorganic phosphates, uric acid, uric acid salts and albumin in adult rabbits due to solid food consumption. When less water is consumed, the urine may appear heavy and white like spackle wall-patching compound (calcium carbonate). Urine may appear deep orange to red when there is an incomplete synthesis of a vitamin nutrient. The pH is not normal, and the urine is alkaline. This does not affect the health of the Lop and is a temporary condition usually due to high protein (alfalfa) food consumption. To dispel any fears you may have, a small amount of vinegar in the water will neutralize the urine should this be the problem. Urinary infections are not common in rabbits.

Examine the genital area of your Lop often in order to catch any abnormalities. Unknowingly, a bladder infection was allowed to worsen in a buck who showed no other symptoms but loss of appetite and weight and a slight swelling and leaking of fluid around the genital area which was not seen in time. The seepage drew flies which led to maggot infestation. At this point, the buck died. Treatment suggested was penicillin injections and the use of a sterile needle to puncture the filled pockets in the genital and tail area. Infected genital areas should be protected by Pet-Guard Gel (an insecticide repellent with lanolin) or something similar, and removing any maggots by the use of ether.

Pinworms are the worms typically found in rabbits and can be seen on the feces as white threads. Sometimes pinworms are not seen, but the Lop will look scruffy over a long period of time. Lops shown at rabbit shows or allowed to run in the yard are more apt to pick up pinworms. I have seen very few cases and believe it is not a common problem with good management. A regular worming program every four to six months is advisable. When in doubt, a fecal examination by a veterinarian is recommended. The most effective treatment is an undiluted, oral dose of Piperazine (usually 1 cc per 5 pounds of body weight) directly into the mouth using a 3 cc syringe while holding the Lop on his back with its head slightly elevated. Repeat this treatment in ten days to break the life cycle of the worm. An alternate method of worming is to add the Piperazine to the drinking water, but the sensitive nose of the Lop usually detects the medication which results in little if any water being consumed. You have little control over this method of treatment since you do not know how much medication will be taken. Piperazine destroys most worms, but not all. Should your Lop need a more specific wormer, a veterinarian can prescribe it.

Abnormal lumps or swelling may mean a hematoma, which is a tumor or swelling containing blood, possibly due to a broken joint or bone. This occurred in a doe who was thought pregnant and showing abnormally sluggish behavior and poor appetite. The swelling in the abdominal area turned out to be a hematoma due to a broken femur (thighbone). The doe had to be put down by the veterinarian.

Abnormal behavior, movement and appetite (paralysis of

the hindquarters and loss of control of urination and defecation) may mean a broken or fractured back or leg. It is quite common for this to happen since the bones are very fragile. Proper handling of the Lop and safe, secure housing is imperative. The Lop's skeletal structure is finer than that of a cat in proportion to body weight, and the Lop when dropped cannot right himself like a cat. A Lop can race across a floor and hit a doorjamb or be frightened in a cage to the point of bouncing off the sides and breaking a leg or back. A broken back can result if hind legs are free to kick when a distraught Lop is held.

The broken leg of a house Lop was successfully repaired by the temporary use of a pin. The veterinarian advised that two things would bring this French Lop through: love and keeping him clean by daily wiping him all over with a damp washcloth, since the Lops take such pride in cleanliness. Today, the buck, Looie, shares a two-story house and bedroom with a spayed doe, Annie, and has no difficulty with wild times and negotiating the steps to their second-story bedroom.

Cortisone injections have been known to help stabilize and relieve the pain of a broken back until the back healed. Laser treatments have proven successful in helping the body repair a broken joint. Depending on the veterinarian, and priorities, a break or fracture may not necessarily mean the end of the road. In an animal suffering from a fracture, it is important, however, to keep the genital area clean as he is unable to perform his normal hygienic rituals and you must prevent hutch burn.

Abnormal movement typifying a paralysis of the legs and head muscles is sometimes called "Head-down Disease" and is caused from milkweed poisoning or the like. Make sure the Lop drinks water. Hold his head or orally administer water through a syringe and feed lots of fruits and vegetables in order to dilute the poison. In extreme cases, call a veterinarian.

Health

EXTERNAL PROBLEMS

Hutch Burn—It is important to periodically check the genital area of the Lop for redness and inflammation caused by bacterial infection as a result of unsanitary conditions. Usually this is seen on does and is caused by a Lop either urinating on herself or urinating in an area and sitting in it. If left unattended during the fly season, the area will draw flies, and maggot infestation may result in the death of the Lop. Wash the affected area with a mild soap like castile or liquid organic, and dry with a towel in warm weather or with a hair dryer set on low in cold weather. An application of Bag Balm (used for exterior udder problems) or Nitro furazone dressing or ointment will heal the area.

Sanitation plays a major role in the health of your Lop and cannot be overemphasized. Poor sanitation and overcrowding has been the ruin of many reputable rabbitries with once healthy, good stock.

A doe may constantly urinate on her sitting board or in her nest box and sit in it. The board should be washed off and turned over and set in a new place, away from the potty corner. The same is true with regard to a nest box. I have seen a doe in need of being bred to the point of constantly urinating on herself and the sitting board. This stopped once the doe was bred. If the doe is not to be bred, this practice can be eliminated with spaying or neutering.

Abscesses (staph infections)—Abscesses occur from bacterial infections when the skin is broken, usually as a result of sore hocks, punctures, scratches and bites. Abscesses will develop if sutured areas are not medicated daily with Nitrofurazone ointment during and after removal of the sutures to prevent the entrance of harmful bacteria through any lesions.

Abscesses feel like knots under the skin and should be lanced with a surgical blade, razor or 18 gauge disposable needle. I find the 18 gauge needle works well for opening large abscesses and the 22 gauge needle works well for small abscesses. Insert the needle into the heart of the abscess, which is usually seen as a whitish area, or head, when the area is squeezed at the base. Withdraw the needle and squeeze at the base of the abscess to bring the cheese-like pus which fills the cavity to the surface through the puncture. You may have to reinsert the needle several times and withdraw with a ripping action up and outwards to increase the size of the opening to allow all the pus to be squeezed out. Abscesses may wall themselves off from adjoining abscesses. Several openings may have to be made and a small hemostat used to break down surrounding tissue to completely empty the matter from the area, thereby eliminating any knot or lump beneath the skin. The openings should be large enough to insert the tip of a 1 cc or 3 cc disposable syringe in order to daily flush out the cavities first with hydrogen peroxide and then with an antibacterial medication such as liquid Nitrofurazone. Nitrofurazone ointment can be used to seal in the liquid.

It is important to allow the abscess pockets to heal from the inside out. It may be necessary to reopen the abscesses daily should they heal over, squeezing out any accumulated pus. Day by day, the cavity will grow smaller and smaller, taking less and less liquid. At the time of the initial incisions, if all the matter is expelled, the area should feel normal, with no knots or lumps. During the days to follow, scar tissue—not abscesses—may be felt, which will dissipate in time. Care should be taken in flushing abscesses in the throat area as the tissue is very delicate and can be ruptured from excess pressure, causing suffocation.

Other medications that are very effective in healing abscesses are Kymar Ointment (Neomycin Palmitate-Hydrocortisone Acetate-Trypsin-Chymotrypsin Concentrate Ointment) which liquefies dead or necrotic tissue, an antibiotic enzyme combination, and Xenodine Polyhydroxydine Solution, more effective than iodine.

In chronic cases, a systemic medication should be given orally so the staph infection will not run rampant throughout the body. I recommend Chloromycetin Palmitate (Chloramphenicol Palmitate Oral Suspension) by Parke-Davis which is given orally two to three times a day (lcc per 6 pounds of body weight). Another effective medication is Keflex (Cephalixin) by Lilly available in three strengths of liquid, the easiest to use being 250 mg./tsp. suspension given orally every eight hours (lcc per 5 pounds of body weight). Keep the medications refrigerated and wash the syringe with water after each dosage.

The aforementioned medications are obtained through a veterinarian.

Rinse all tools with water after use, except the syringe used for hydrogen peroxide and Nitrofurazone. I use two small shot glasses, one for the hydrogen peroxide and one for the Nitrofurazone or Xenodine as needed. I then flush the syringe out with hydrogen peroxide, empty the excess hydrogen peroxide, Nitrofurazone liquid or Xenodine from the glasses and wipe them out with a paper towel. The syringe is stored in a clean place until further use on the same animal.

The needle, razor or surgical blade should be further cleaned with alcohol. Since alcohol does not kill all germs, an iodine cleanser like Betadine Skin Cleanser, Betadine Solution, Xenodine or straight iodine should be used. I store the needle used in a small shot glass filled with Betadine Solution for a short time should it be needed to reopen abscessed pockets on the same animal.

It is important to remember not to use the same disposable needles or syringes on different animals. Throw them away when treatment is over. Thoroughly clean and disinfect other instruments used, such as a surgical blade and glasses. Use separate glasses for the different animals treated.

Health

Treat problem animals after working with healthy animals and wash hands thoroughly using Betadine Skin Cleanser. A change of clothing is recommended after treatment to help prevent the spread of bacteria.

Sore Hocks—Due to the rapid growth of the large Lop, the hocks may not have a chance to toughen in sufficient time to keep the wire floor from becoming a big irritant. Unsanitary conditions where urine, etc., penetrates the hock fur and burns the skin may cause sore hocks which will more likely than not cause abscesses. Rough or rusty floor wire or salt-coated wire resulting from a salt spool merely placed on the floor wire will traumatize the hocks. Also, a Lop that stomps about because of harassment or is hyperactive by nature or has long nails is a good candidate for sore hocks.

When sore hocks are detected, trim off excessive nail length and wash the hocks with mild soap and water, should they be urine stained. When dry, apply a blue lotion containing Tincture Benzoin and Tanaic and Salicylic Acid, which is an antiseptic that toughens skin and is used on hunting dogs (Blue Foot). Extra sitting boards and a layer of straw on the floor helps the healing process. Remove wet and/or dirty straw daily.

Iodine and iodine-based medications may also be used as antibacterial/antifungal medications. If there are abscesses, treat as described for abscesses.

Wet Dewlap (bacterial and fungal infections)—During the summer months or days of high humidity, both bucks and does can pick up a chronic moist dermatitis resulting in a bacterial and/or fungal infection with loss of fur on face, dewlap, chin, legs and/or feet. In does, it is commonly known as a wet dewlap. In bucks, I refer to it as fungus face. Extremely high humidity promotes disease, staph and fungal infections.

Fungal and/or bacterial infections are caused by continuous wetting of fur, usually from drinking out of or wallowing in the water crock. Sometimes an infection may not be obvious. I discovered this problem because of an unusual depression in a Lop. Check the neck area and chin for possible abscesses which can result from excessive scratching of the area affected. Sometimes a bacterial/fungal infection which appears slimy and/or green may emerge on the side of the mouth and face of a Lop.

If the problem is a wet dewlap, you can place a small rubber ball in the water or raise the crock using a wire hanger or crock holder or replace the crock with a one-half gallon pickle crock which is high enough to keep the dewlap from becoming wet. If the area affected is the nose, lip, face, chin or feet, then remove the crock and replace it with a rabbit water bottle. You may have to squeeze the bottle to emit water should the Lop not know what to do. If a lactating doe refuses to drink out of a water bottle, you may have to supplement the intake manually, using a syringe to prevent dehydration and no milk production.

Any slimy fur should be cut away using rounded-tipped grooming or bandage scissors. If the skin is raw, Betadine Ointment is good to use as the iodine in it will kill the fungus. You can also apply a baby powder, corn starch or fungus powder to dry the area. Be careful not to allow the Lop to inhale the powder. Iodine or a prescribed antifungal cream like Conofite (Miconazole Nitrate) applied to affected areas will also stop the spread of a fungal infection, especially on the legs and between the toes.

A wet dewlap during cold weather can lead to a respiratory problem, so remedy the problem immediately. Treatment is best done with the Lop held on his back in a reclining position. Be careful when cutting fur as the skin is so thin and supple that it is very easy to cut it in error.

Sore or Weepy Eyes (ears)—Redness and sores in the inner corners of the eyes are usually the result of head and ear scratching. Unseen wax deep within the ear can build up and cause secondary infections. Use a nongreasy, nonoily cleaning solution such as OtiClean-A for periodic, general cleaning. This type of cleaner is excellent to use before shows because it does not leave a greasy residue on ears and crown. These cleaning solutions may be procured through a veterinarian.

For acute, secondary infections of the ear, Panalog Ointment, Tresaderm, Liquichlor, and Gentocin are effective and are obtained through a veterinarian.

Always check the size of the ear canals to make sure the passages are open and not swollen.

Ears may show dirt, wax and/or crust, a sign of mite infestation. Using an eyedropper or other small applicator, place several drops of heavy mineral oil in the ear, filling the canal, and massage the outside of the ear canal with the thumb and index finger in an upward and downward motion. The oil will smother any mites and bring to the surface any scale and wax not visible. Let the Lop shake his head, swab with wood stick cotton swabs and repeat the procedure until no more matter is brought to the surface. Repeat treatment in six to ten days in order to break the mite cycle. I find using a four-ounce plastic bottle with a flip-top nozzle is very helpful in dispensing the mineral oil. Tresaderm, Xenodine and Veltrim are medications found effective against mite infestation; they are obtained through a veterinarian.

Skin Mites—Check behind the head and across the shoulders for signs of mites. The skin may appear red, the fur thin or missing and scabs and scale obvious in this area when mites are posing an annoying problem. A cat flea powder or garden/dog and cat pesticide powder will safely eliminate the skin mite problem. Usually any medication used on cats can safely be used on Lops because they share the same thin, sensitive skin. Do not use a flea collar on Lops as they do not accept anything around the neck.

Pour the dust or powder in your hand and then apply it to the Lop in the areas where it is needed, being careful the

Lop does not inhale too much dust. Repeat the following day and as often as needed until the irritation disappears and new fur growth is evident. I have heard of only one allergic reaction to this treatment which resulted in sneezing and runny, watery eyes and nose.

Dandruff-A severe case of dandruff along the spine is sometimes seen during a moult and responds well to a cat flea powder or garden/dog and cat pesticide powder applied as recommended for skin mites.

Weepy Eyes—Eye irritation may be attributed to drafty conditions, airborne dirt or pollen, allergies, ammonia fumes, blocked tear ducts or ulcerations. Treat eyes with Terramycin eye ointment (ophthalmic) or a boric acid solution.

Blocked tear ducts result in clear fluid overflowing the lower eye lid. A milky discharge is evident when a secondary bacterial infection is present. Blocked tear ducts can result from several causes. The most common is because of the desired bulldog head and fat cheeks seen on many Lops.

Secondary infections have been successfully treated with ophthalmic ointments containing Chloramphenicol such as Chloricol and Neomycin-based ophthalmic medications such as Mycitracin and Anaprime obtained through a veterinarian. The duct can also be flushed out by a veterinarian in conjunction with the use of an eye medication. Use of a nasal decongestant spray together with an eye medication has proven effective in some cases.

A veterinarian will be able to detect an ulceration and prescribe the proper medication. Ointments containing cortisone should not be used when the eye is ulcerated.

Hutch burn and sore hocks on this Lop show why sanitation is so important. (Below): Surgical tools you will need, clockwise from the top: surgical blade with handle (dissecting knife), 1 cc. syringe in shot glass, 3 cc. disposable syringe, hemostat, and two 22 gauge ¾" disposable needles (one in a case).

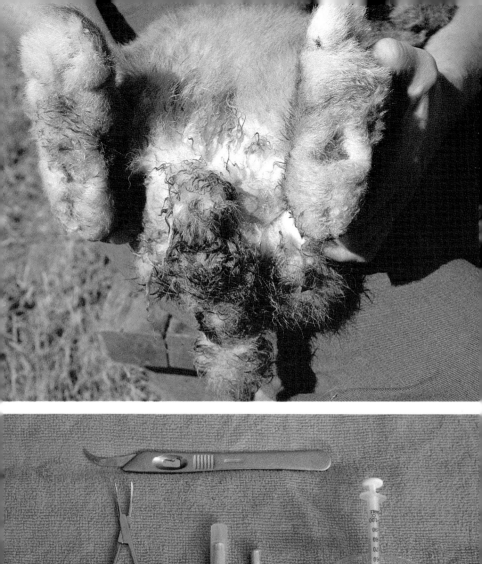

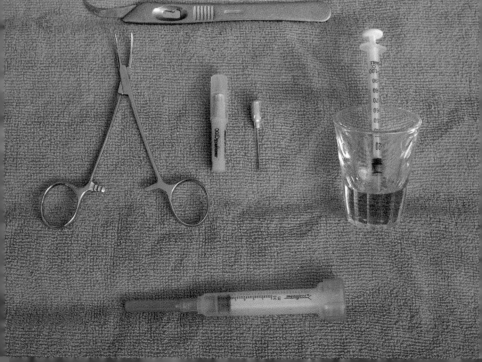

Health

Conjunctivitis—A chronic eye infection involving inflammation of the eyelids is usually a symptom of Pasteurella Multocida. Treat with ophthalmic ointments containing sulfonamides, antibiotics, or antibiotics and a steroid. Recurrence is common and if that is the case, the Lop should be put down (euthanized) in the best interest of the Lop and the welfare of other rabbits.

Entropion—Inversion of the eyelid (entropion) may be an inherited defect and is sometimes seen in Lops. Entropion may be secondary to another problem which makes the eyelids swell, causing the eyelashes to turn inward and irritate the cornea, thus producing pain and infection. If genetic, the problem can be corrected through surgery, but the Lop so affected should not be used for breeding.

What has been more recently seen in the Lop is what is termed "Notched" Entropion, which affects one or both upper lids and involves a few eyelashes giving a notched appearance. Treatment with any ophthalmic ointment is recommended to help relieve pain and irritation in an effort to avoid eye inflammation and ulceration. A white spot appearing on the eye is a sign of inflammation, but not necessarily ulceration. A veterinarian will be able to detect an ulceration and prescribe the proper medication. Lops with this type of Entropion will outgrow this condition, but it is important to treat the affected eyes until that time which may be several weeks.

, *Cuterebra Larvae*—Small bumps on the body may result from the larvae of the adult Cuterebra fly burrowing into the skin. It attaches itself with two mouth hooks. Pus and

Upper photo: This Lop is sneezing. Sneezing may be caused by an allergy and is not necessarily a symptom of anything serious at all. Lower photo: Constable's Superstar, 18-month-old tortoiseshell Grand Champion, exhibiting ear control during stress.

blood may pass from a breathing hole made through the skin by the parasite. The larvae remains under the skin until it is approximately ¾ of an inch long by 3/8 of an inch wide at which time it emerges from the host and drops to the ground where it will pupate.

Remove the larva by making three short cuts with a sterile instrument cutting from the larva outwards. Do not cut into the larva. Grasp the end of the larva and pull out. The midsection of the larva is larger than the ends (the reason for three incisions). Squeeze out all pus and flush out with hydrogen peroxide using a small syringe. Administer liquid Nitrofurazone. Repeat daily until the cavity heals from the inside out.

Fur Chewing or Eating—A Lop eating another's fur and/or his own may mean several things: a protein deficiency, a lack of roughage or an inherited behavior pattern. The inherited behavior pattern has been observed in some Holland and Mini Lops. If large amounts of fur are eaten, there may be a blockage. Therefore, feed plenty of hay regardless of the cause.

Spraddle or Splay Legs—This condition may develop in young Lops which grow very rapidly, thus weakening bones, muscles and tendons. It may be a hereditary weakness, a nutritional deficiency or an injury from a blundering doe. The legs spread away from the body, prohibiting movement. Excessive heat from the wire on hot days can cause this condition. When one front leg on a very young Lop is affected, it may be caused by trauma such as dropping from a height, as out of the nest box. Rear legs may be affected due to hip joint damage by does during difficult labor. It is important to keep the food intake regulated on fast-growing, ravenous Lops,

Black junior English Lop buck. (Below): Sable point senior Mini Lop doe and frosty point junior Holland Lop doe.

possibly eliminating any high-energy additives. Keep wire cages from overheating during extremely hot days. Keep a stepping stone or cushion of hay in front of a nest box at all times to avoid leg injuries on overactive babies. For the welfare of the animal extreme cases should be put down.

Heat Prostration—Sneezing and nasal discharge may be due to acute perspiration from the nose on extremely hot days or in uncomfortably warm confines. Symptoms of heat prostration are rapid breathing, wetness around the nose and mouth, drooling, and possibly slight bleeding from the nose. Usually the Lop is stretched out on his stomach with head tipped back. Ear blood vessels become greatly enlarged and the mouth will turn blue in the latter stages. Obese Lops, pregnant and nursing does and kits in the nest box with excessive bedding and poor ventilation are extremely susceptible to heat prostration.

In extremely hot weather, it is best to locate your Lop in the coolest part of the house or yard. Outside, shade trees are preferred. If none are available, burlap extended from the roof along the sides of the hutch and a soaker hose emitting water on top of the roof, wetting the burlap, will reduce the temperature of the immediate area. The Lop will use the water crock to cool his ears, which are his ventilating system.

A fogger system consisting of fogger heads inserted into ½ inch PVC pipe (plastic) on the roof of a building or hutch creates a mist or fog and evaporation is the cooling agent. The fogger system can be turned on automatically by using a solenoid valve wired into a thermostat to automatically turn on and off the fogger when the temperature reaches or falls below selected degrees. The moisture from the foggers evaporates before it can blow into the building or hutches.

Two views of a broken fawn senior Holland Lop buck.

Health

Also, large buildings have been cooled using cellulose-filled padding located at one end of the rabbitry and kept wet by trickling water. Fans pull air into the building and through the padding and out the opposite end of the building. This evaporative cooling system requires a tightly closed building to be effective.

Placing large blocks of ice or one-half gallon milk cartons containing frozen water next to the water crocks will not only reduce the water temperature, but will be an effective air conditioner as the Lop rests against them. A small plastic bottle of frozen water works well in the nest box, but make sure the babies do not get wet and are placed near and not on the bottle. Wet towels in lieu of ice-filled containers can be placed on the sitting boards and kept wet throughout the day. The towels must be taken away when the temperature drops, to prevent a chilled, wet Lop at nightfall. Water-soaked bricks and tiles also have been used successfully. Do not worry if the Lop eats the milk carton. Keep plastic, rubber and foil from his digestive tract.

Electrolytes (Hydro-Lite) in the water are a must to prevent dehydration. Do not forget to have a salt spool readily available.

In case of heat prostration, submerge the Lop in tepid water. Be careful not to drop the body temperature too low, thus severely shocking the body. Heat prostration is difficult to treat and usually fatal, so the use of preventive measures can not be overstressed.

Maggot Infestation—Always check your Lop for any sores or dirty matter, in the genital area especially, during the hot weather. An oversight can mean maggot infestation within 24 hours. Ether will kill maggots and can be obtained

Senior Mini Lop agouti doe. (Below): A Holland Lop and Mini Lop playing.

through some drug stores, usually upon prescription by a veterinarian. A container of ether can be stored in the refrigerator in a covered coffee can to control fumes, evaporation, and combustion. It is not often that veterinarians have ether on hand. Clip and clean the area and soak if necessary in a solution of Betadine and water (half and half). Apply Nitrofurazone ointment and an insecticide repellent to deter the flies. Treat the infected area daily until healed.

Syphilis—Called Vent Disease, syphilis is a venereal disease of domestic rabbits. The genital area becomes ulcerated and covered with a heavy scab. Small lesions may be found on the lips and/or eyelids. Transmission of the disease to both sexes is by mating. The lesions heal, but the Lop is a carrier unless treated and cured with penicillin injections. Do not use a synthetic penicillin on rabbits.

A latent Vent Disease can cause abortions with loss of litters from the 22nd day of gestation to term, with no obvious symptoms.

Myxomatosis—Myxomatosis is a fatal viral disease of the rabbit transmitted by mosquitoes, biting flies and direct contact. It is usually found in the coastal area of California and Oregon, where epidemics occur every eight to ten years during the summer months. Young up to a month old appear more resistant to the disease than older animals.

Symptoms are acute conjunctivitis, listlessness, loss of appetite and high fever, frequently reaching 108°F. Some will die in 48 hours while others become progressively depressed, develop a rough coat, and the eyelids, nose, lips and ears become swollen. The genitalia becomes inflamed and swollen. A pussy nasal discharge appears, breathing

Two views of a lovely sable point Senior Mini Lop doe.

becomes labored and a coma results just before death, which usually occurs within one to two weeks after the appearance of the conjunctivitis. Animals that linger on longer usually develop fibrotic nodules on the nose, ears and forefeet. A live vaccine prepared from a weakened Myxomatosis virus has been used to protect rabbits. Good rabbit management and the elimination of breeding grounds of mosquitoes and flies is advised.

Ketosis (Pregnancy Toxemia)—Obesity and lack of exercise may result in the death of does at kindling or a day or two before kindling. Does should be fed according to size and kept in cages large enough to afford the proper exercise for fitness.

Ear Injuries—The Lop rabbit is very prone to ear damage, especially the English Lop. Severe hemorrhage and blood loss can result in death from eight to twelve hours after injury. Otherwise, with continued blood loss over a long period of time, the result is anemia and systemic body infection. Direct pressure on the wound will usually control the bleeding. Suturing by a veterinarian may be needed but end tissue will usually dry and slough.

Loss of Equilibrium—Total loss of equilibrium may follow signs of Wry Neck with the head abnormally positioned to the side. With loss of control of locomotor functions and paralysis or incoordination of all four limbs, the Lop may continually roll about in an uncontrollable fashion. This may result from an extension of an upper respiratory infection or acute inner ear infection associated with Pasteurella. Wry Neck is very difficult to treat. Terramycin ear medication has been successful in some cases, but symptoms usually recur.

Depicting the rare, recessive colors, from left to right: broken blue, lynx and broken opal. These are all six-week-old English Lops.

Medications

The *Merck Veterinary Manual,* which is a handbook of diagnosis and therapy for veterinarians, is a very helpful book with regard to diseases and medications of animals. More up-to-date information can be obtained from *The Journal of Applied Rabbit Research* published periodically by Oregon State University Rabbit Research Center, Corvallis, Oregon 97331, and available to supporters. Omaha Vaccine Company, Inc., P.O. Box 7228, 3030 "L" Street, Omaha, Nebraska 68107, is a source of medications by mail order catalog.

ORAL MEDICATIONS

It is difficult to control the exact dosage of oral medications when added to the drinking water, and absorption is much slower than with injected medications. Some medications irritate the stomach and intestines, causing intestinal upset and possibly diarrhea. Some are rendered ineffective by digestive enzymes before entering the blood stream and form complexes with ingested food and are never absorbed from the digestive tract. Some antibacterial medications eliminate beneficial bacteria as well as the harmful bacteria of the gastro-intestinal tract which leads to severe intestinal complications possibly resulting in death. Therefore, it is recommended that medication be administered to ill or sick animals only and not indiscriminately as a preventive measure.

(Top, left): Though still tiny, this month-old chocolate Holland Lop exhibits the body type it will possess at maturity. (Top, right): This is a six-month-old Holland Lop buck. (Bottom, left): Ten-month-old blue Holland Lop buck weighing four pounds. (Bottom, right): Blue fawn English Lop at six-weeks of age.

Medications

INJECTABLE MEDICATIONS

Absorption into the blood stream is much faster with injectable medications, but proper procedure is imperative to avoid undesirable side effects.

Always use a sterile needle and syringe. Usually the disposable needles used for intramuscular injections are 22 gauge by 1 inch for fluid medications and 20 or 18 gauge by 1 inch for heavier medications, attached to a 3 cc disposable syringe. One-half inch long disposable needles should be used for subcutaneous injections.

The medication of a subcutaneous (Sub-Q) injection is deposited in the tissue between the skin and the muscle. Some drugs may cause severe tissue reaction and sloughing of the skin.

To withdraw the desired amount of medication into the syringe, you should inject an equal amount of air into the vial of medication and then aspirate (draw by suction) the medication into the syringe. While holding the filled syringe with needle pointing upward, tap out any air bubbles trapped in the medication prior to injection. The air bubbles will escape through the needle.

The best site for subcutaneous injections is just behind the elbow joint. A fold of skin over the area should be grasped between the thumb and forefinger (left hand for right-handed persons) and pulled away from the body, forming a tent and space between the skin and muscle. The needle with syringe, held in the opposite hand, is quickly inserted through the skin against the lay of the fur and into the center of the tent. After the needle is placed in the skin, aspirate (pull back the plunger on the syringe). If blood ap-

(Top, left): Judge Carl Earl looking for thick, dense fur with good roll-back on this Madagascar French Lop. (Top, right): The outstanding feature of this English Lop being examined is its long ears. (Bottom): Checking the ears on this English Lop for its tattoo.

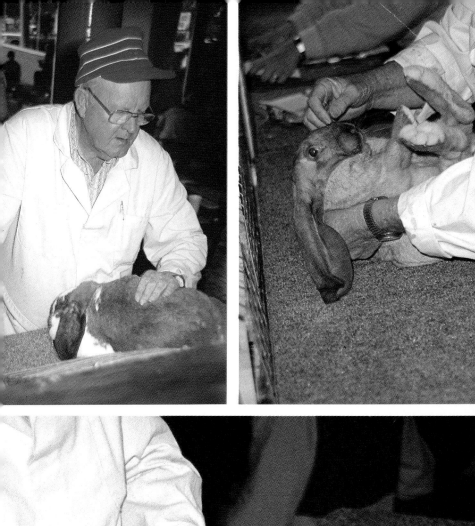
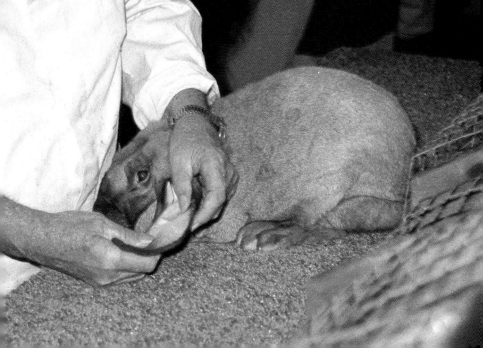

pears in the barrel of the syringe, withdraw the needle completely and reinsert the needle again because the blood indicates the needle has entered a vein. Afterwards, aspirate again, and if no blood appears, gently push in the plunger, depositing the medication beneath the skin. Remove the needle with one quick motion.

Intramuscular injections are absorbed more rapidly into the blood stream than subcutaneous injections. The two most common sites for intramuscular injections are the back of the rear leg (thigh) or the lumbar (loin) muscle of the back. I do not use the rear leg for injections as there is the possibility of injuring one of the major nerves to the rear foot.

The best site for intramuscular injections is one and one-half inches behind the last rib and one-half to one inch away from the spine (three finger widths from the last rib and two finger widths down from the spine), the thickest part of the loin muscle. After the site of injection has been determined, place pressure at the site with the index finger of your free hand and insert the needle at the tip of the index finger into the center of the loin muscle. Aspirate the syringe. If no blood appears, slowly inject the medication into the muscle.

When in doubt or reluctant, work with a veterinarian on the above procedures.

USE OF MEDICATIONS

It is important to keep in the blood the level of any medication high enough for a long period of time in order for it to be effective. If symptoms disappear, continue use of the medication for the prescribed length of time, usually for five days.

Mr. Crook's wonderful photo of a begging Lop!

Medications

Indiscriminate use of a medication will render it ineffective in generations to come because an immunity or resistance will develop.

Synthetic penicillins such as Ampicillin and Amoxicillin should not be used on rabbits, due to adverse effects such as loss of appetite.

Some medications antagonize or cancel the effects of another. Do not use Combiotic (Pencillin-Streptomycin) with Terramycin.

I do not recommend the use of medicated feed because it is not a cure, but a crutch and contributes to the making of antibiotic-resistant bacteria.

Prolonged use of sulfa medications can cause kidney damage.

Do not overdose antibiotics as it will alter the digestive bacterial flora, producing fatal diarrhea.

When in doubt, find a lab to perform a culture/sensitivity test to be sure what the problem is and what drugs will or will not help.

Antibacterial Therapeutic Agent Combinations.

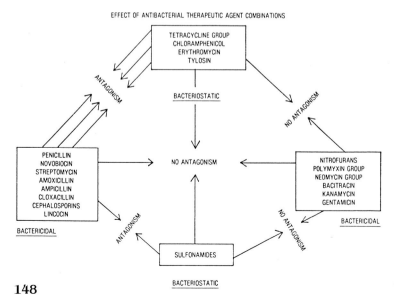

(Top, left to right): Broken fawn senior Holland Lop buck. Courtesy of the "Five A Double Bar Bunny Ranch"; Grand Champion chinchilla senior Mini Lop doe, Sandee's Gardenia. Courtesy of "Hoppin' Posie Loppitry." (Bottom, left to right): Tortoiseshell senior English Lop doe. Courtesy of "Eden's Olde English Rabbitry"; Broken Madagascar senior French Lop doe. Courtesy of Crook's Lophouse.

Breeding

It is important as a breeder to improve upon the genetics of the Lops, not only with regard to the ARBA Standard, but also with regard to temperament, health and maternal qualities. With the prime purpose being pet and fancy and not meat and fur, you've lost everything if you lose temperament and health. Whether you have one Lop or many Lops, or breed once or many times, you are still a breeder, and doing the best by what you have is of the utmost importance. The show table gives direction to a breeding program, but to breed strictly for the show table, regardless of the cost to the Lop is an injustice to the animal for self-reward. You would be better breeding a meat or fur breed if sweepstakes points is your motivation, as temperament and health unfortunately are not prime considerations with them.

Regardless, do not breed Lops too young or if there are genetic defects.

Do not breed for cuteness or for the purpose of letting children or adults experience the miracle of birth. If that is the case, try to visit a rabbitry for entertainment.

Do not breed for added income. You may not have the same quality stock or access to the same customers as another breeder.

Do not breed unless you are willing to protect your Lops with a respectable price since it is human nature not to care for something obtained too easily.

The top animal's genitalia are those of a male; the bottom is a female.

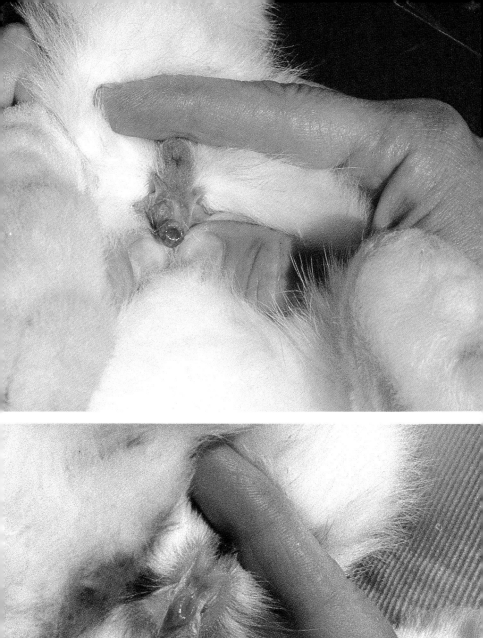
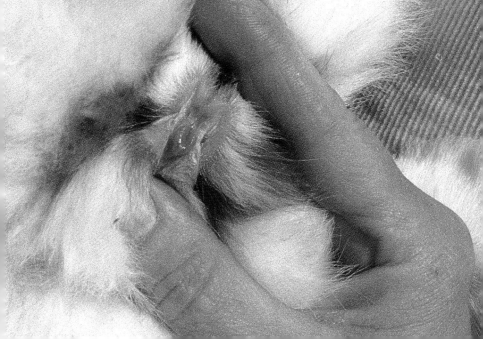

Breeding

Please remember that there are too many unwanted animals, born because people did not stop to think, and these animals are living and dying inhumanely. The majority of the animals needlessly destroyed at humane societies are victims of thoughtless breeders who resorted to abandoning, giving away or selling cheap a living creature with feelings.

There is much work and hardship involved in being a good breeder of Lops. A breeder will have great Lops as well as Lops that may have to be destroyed or euthanized in the best interest of the animal because of a deformity, malocclusion, or the like. When you go to great lengths to do it right, you will find that you are a breeder for the love of the Lop, since expenses outweigh the income.

If you have decided to become a breeder, obtain as much literature as you can through the American Rabbit Breeders Association, your respective breed club at the national and local level, book and feed stores and libraries. Always feel free to seek the help of the breeder you bought your animals from, as every breeder knows his or her animals best and knows what you are dealing with.

GENETICS

A breeding pair should complement each other, as the offspring will carry the combined genes or characteristics of the parents. Therefore, if there is a problem of length in the doe, breed her to a short-bodied buck to offset the fault. If the buck is short, but fails in the shoulders (flat shoulders being a common problem), breed to a doe with excellent shoulders. Breeding short loin to short loin will result in lesser weight and size.

These French Lops are mating. The male (buck) mounts the doe in the upper photo. After a successful mating, he falls to the side as shown in the lower photo.

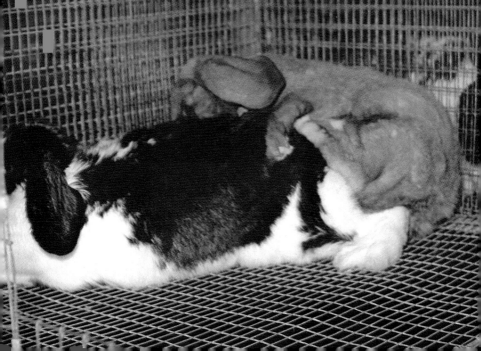

Breeding

With regard to disposition, does have been known to be a bit temperamental when in season or during pregnancy. Usually the worst behavior has proven to be strong instincts of a good, protective mother who mellows to a love, once motherhood has been experienced successfully. I look to the buck and to the doe's littermates for the quality of disposition, body type, etc., and make decisions accordingly. The reverse can be said of a standoffish buck. I look at the disposition, body type and the like of his littermates, and then breed to the best doe with regard to disposition, should there be any doubts. I am not talking about a mean, terrifying Lop with regard to disposition problems. Such Lops should be checked over for physical problems, such as acute ear infections, which may be the cause of unnatural behavior. If the consensus is a mean animal, he should be humanely destroyed and the genetic line eliminated.

Genes are either dominant or recessive or partially dominant, as seen in color. The dominant genes for a specific trait will cancel the recessive genes in the mate and the offspring will have that particular dominant trait. The effect of recessive genes is seen when two pair up and there are no dominant genes to hide them.

Certain characteristics or traits may be influenced by many genes, which is a polygenic inheritance. Such is the case with regard to malocclusion. It has been believed that some malocclusion is recessive in inheritance. Recent experiments dispel this theory. Malocclusion is believed to be polygenic. One experiment involved two rabbits with confirmed cases of malocclusion who produced normal offspring.

(Top, left): Wooden nest boxes, such as the one shown here, provide the best insulation against heat and cold for the kits. (Top, right): Eight-day-old kits are blind and deaf. (Bottom): A mother Lop's view of the kits in her nest box.

Breeding

Color and pattern are affected by genes. Lop colors compare closely to those of the Netherland Dwarf. Some of the colors are albino, black, agouti, steel, fawn, sooty fawn, tortoiseshell (Madagascar), blue, opal, chinchilla, frosty point, chocolate point, seal point, lynx, squirrel (blue chinchilla) and chocolate. New colors are becoming available. The rare colors come from dilute genes. You will get a lot of black Lops when breeding rare colors, but black is needed to keep colors rich.

The agouti (banded) color, which resembles the color of a wild rabbit, is a blend of the effects of three groups of genes. The normal band width is a dominant gene (about 1/5 " or 5 mm) and the wide band width is a recessive gene which doubles the width. Intensity or amount of color (fawn or black pigment) is controlled by genes. The yellow (fawn) band appears almost chestnut in an agouti when a lot of yellow pigment is present. Lops appear washed out or gray when there is very little yellow pigment present. Genes control the placement of the band in relation to the black tip. An agouti appears darker with a large black tip, more so than when the band is near the tip.

In steels, there is a gene that narrows the width of the band in the fur. One steel gene is responsible for the normal steel banding. Breeding two steels together is not desirable as some of the offspring will inherit a steel gene from each parent. This occurs approximately 25% of the time and causes the band width to narrow to the point of disappearing, except behind the neck or on the flanks. This produces the bad or dirty blacks.

An assistant is necessary when tattooing. (Bottom): Registrar Frances Booth checking a just-completed tattoo in the right ear of a French Lop.

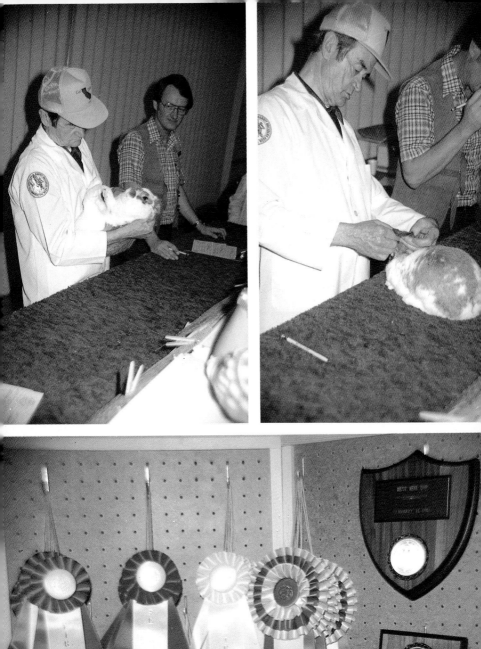

Breeding

Odd or rare colors brought about by dilute, recessive genes are the result of intense breeding programs pooling or combining such genes. This may lead to poor, washed-out, or unusual, attractive colors not recognized by the ARBA. Some genetic abnormalities linked to dilute color genes have been apparent because of retarded growth in kits where the ears curl and the stomach grows to the point where the young Lop cannot walk around correctly with legs paddling like a turtle. It seems that the food consumed is not assimilated and the Lop usually dies before long. It is humane to euthanize the Lop when movement seems to be inhibited.

Some lines of Siamese colored Lops have been known to be unusually small and short-lived and have problems reproducing themselves.

Chocolates (what some people may call sables) seem to be the link to the Siamese and other unusual colors.

Dilute Black = Tortoiseshell or Madagascar, Blue, Chocolate

Double Dilute Black = Frosty, Chocolate (Sable) and Seal Points Lilac

Dilute Agouti = Fawn or Sooty Fawn, Steel, Chinchilla

Double Dilute Agouti = Red Fawn (Red), Cream

Lynx (Blue Cream), Opal

Genes producing the chinchilla color may produce blacks ticked with white hairs when combined with non-agouti or non-banded genes. When these black/chinchilla Lops are bred to Lops carrying a gene masking the black pigment, the result is the Siamese color.

Judge Forrest Harper judging. He examines a Mini Lop carefully while a clerk records his remarks. Then he checks the ear tattoo. Finally, bottom photo, the awards!

Breeding

There is a gene responsible for the white markings on the Lops. When two of these genes combine, more white is found in the pattern which is known as parti-colored or Charlie. Therefore, generally it is not advisable to breed broken to broken as the correct pattern is generally lost. Also, there is a group of genes responsible for the placement of the white in Lops. Parti-colored Lops or Charlies many times are of excellent type and should be used in a breeding program bred to self Lops with tight pattern genes or to assure brokens in a first litter. (Charlies bred to selfs produce 100% broken litters.)

Another way proven to be successful in producing uniform markings is to linebreed two brokens which have the desired markings. This will produce what is termed an "F_1" generation of 25% selfs, 50% brokens and 25% parti. Then select the best-bodied self and inbreed him to the best-bodied parti. This will produce 100% brokens in what is termed an "F_2" litter and the patterns should be more uniform. You can then continue linebreeding the F_2 to the grandparents.

Partial dominant genes with regard to color partially block out the effects of other genes, thus resulting in variation of color intensity such as a light chinchilla, medium chinchilla and dark chinchilla color. The Siamese colors (frosty point, chocolate point and seal point) correspond to the three chinchilla color genes as these colors are the result of the elimination of the black pigment in the chinchilla due to modifying genes.

In attempting to produce color by using a Lop of the desired color bred to another colored Lop, the litter may not show the color desired, but will produce the desired color if bred back to the parent of the desired color (inbreeding).

Also, much variability will be seen within a litter with regard to growth rates and balance, due to the mixing of lines and this variability will be seen to a lesser and lesser extent with linebreeding.

160

Breeding

BREEDING PROGRAMS

There are three types of programs or plans to follow when breeding: Outbreeding, Linebreeding and Inbreeding.

Outbreeding is the mating of two unrelated Lops of the same breed and is used to introduce new traits and stamina to a breeding line. Breed to combine good type, good milking and maternal traits, and good temperament into a hardy animal. It will take several years to breed uniformity of quality into the line. Runts may not be "runts," but the result of different growth rates due to gene variability in a litter.

Outbreeding may cause a temporary and sometimes permanent malocclusion in offspring due to a difference in head types, etc. Early checking of the teeth, especially at three weeks, and clipping of teeth if need be, will help realign the teeth to proper occlusion as the rapid growth rates of the kits realigns the jaws. Breeding offspring back to the desired parent or to Lops with similar head shapes will eliminate the problem by fixing traits within one or two generations.

It is recommended to introduce new bloodlines or genes to your lines through a doe instead of a buck. Good and bad traits are introduced through outbreeding and the number of offspring is less overwhelming, allowing for a more controlled evaluation with the introduction of a new doe bred to your best buck. This eliminates the tendency to breed the new buck to every doe in the herd and possibly cause a setback in a previously good, conservative breeding program.

Linebreeding is the mating of two Lops of the same breed who are related and are close descendants of a mutual outstanding ancestor. Linebreeding is commonly practiced to perpetuate good qualities. Mating grandsire to granddaughter, granddam to grandson, uncle to niece and cousins are forms of linebreeding which strengthen

161

desirable characteristics and at the same time bring forth recessive traits which may be desirable or undesirable. Mating Lops from two different lines of linebred stock often produces a single generation with an accelerated growth rate and improved stamina. When purchasing breeding stock, it is wise to allow the breeder to help you choose stock with linebreeding in mind.

Inbreeding is the mating of two Lops closely related such as brother to sister, sire to daughter and dam to son and is frowned upon for the novice as it is a more drastic method of fixing desirable and undesirable characteristics in a very short period of time. Extensive inbreeding over five or six generations may bring forth genetic defects such as malocclusion, abnormal fur and bone, poor balance, lowered resistance to disease and/or infection, and reduction in litter size and fertility. When this occurs, breed to eliminate these faults by outcrossing two Lops devoid of these defects. These problems because of much inbreeding are much easier to eliminate than those incurred because of much outbreeding.

Linebreeding and inbreeding reduces the size of the gene pool to the point where certain desired genes exist and the Lop is prepotent and capable of producing his kind. Early in these programs, with more diverse gene pools, first generation crosses may be very disappointing and worse than the sire and dam. It is recommended to breed the most complementary offspring back to the sire or dam whose line you are developing.

Remember, the best breeding program cannot succeeed if you do not care for your Lops properly and have PATIENCE.

BREEDING PROCEDURES

It is important to breed Lops of age, in good condition and with a good disposition that will not increase the probability of disease or pose a management problem. Breed a self to a self (solid color) or a broken color to a self to preserve good pattern in the brokens.

Breeding season in a natural environment is in spring and early summer. My French Lops conceive from January through August. The neutral season is fall and winter. (I have yet to go through November without having every doe bred more than once and praying for the Christmas litters to arrive in time.)

Lops are capable of conception as young as three months of age, but this is not an advisable age to breed. It is recommended that Holland and Mini Lop breeding programs commence no earlier than six months of age. Holland Lop does should be larger than bucks for easier kindling and larger litters. French and English Lops should not be bred earlier than six or seven months of age. Bucks can usually be used for service a month younger than the does, but should be protected from overaggressive does.

Do not let does become heavy or reach a year or more before breeding for the first time. Fat does usually have problems conceiving, and kindling can prove fatal. If you feel down into the fur over the shoulder and it feels soft and mushy with loose skin, chances are the doe is too fat and there is fat over the ovaries. Therefore, eggs released cannot get to the oviduct to be fertilized because of excess fat. Internal fat around the reproductive organs of a doe accumulates with age regardless of her weight and may cause sterility. Breeding a doe too young results in abnormalities in the litter, should it survive, and physically weakens the doe, resulting in a stunted, short-lived animal.

Does do not have a regular heat cycle and there is no discharge. Does can be bred about 13 out of 16 days. During the three off-days, they are incapable of conception. Checking the vent of the doe will help determine if she will be receptive during breeding. A moist, bright pink to red enlarged vent is preferred over a pale pink or purplish color. The cycle starts with a pale flesh or pink color and ends with a deep purple color. The cycle can be brought about through the act of mating, being mounted by another animal or tactile stimulation. Eggs are shed eight to ten hours after the doe is stimulated. It is wise, therefore, to repeat the breeding about eight hours later to take advantage of the eggs available for fertilization, whether or not the initial breeding was successful. This may also increase the litter size by one or two kits.

Additionally, it is helpful to breed two or more does at the same time so that if one fails to produce an adequate milk supply, another doe can be used as a backup.

A doe that has previously kindled and has failed to conceive for an extended period of time may have had, or still has a uterine infection or metritis caused by a retained placenta or fetus following kindling. It is advisable to see your veterinarian for treatment of metritis.

When the temperature rises over 85 degrees for five days or more, older bucks may become temporarily sterile for up to 90 days. Young bucks between five and seven months of age are not as severely affected by the heat.

A buck whose testicles have not descended (cryptorchidism) will not have live sperm or is sterile because the internal body temperature of the buck is too warm for sperm production. Cryptorchidism can be unilateral (testicles not descended on one side) or bilateral (testicles not descended on both sides) and may be hereditary. Bilateral cryptorchidism renders a buck sterile. Unilateral cryptorchidism has no effect upon the fertility of the buck. Therefore, a buck can sire offspring with only one testicle. Contrary to popular belief, a withered or shriveled scrotum does not mean sterility.

Since a doe is very territorial, she should be brought to the buck's hutch or cage. Remove the sitting board and crocks of food and water in case of spraying or chase. After allowing a short getting-to-know-you period, you may need to correctly position the doe with one hand beneath her

DOE PERFORMANCE RECORD

Buck	Date Bred	Date Due	Date Tested	Date Kindled	Number of Young Born	Left	Added	Raised	Died	Bucks	Does

from the side, elevating her haunches while moving her tail up over her back with the free hand and then quickly repositioning that hand to steady her at the shoulders. If the buck decides to mount the doe's head, he should be repositioned immediately to avoid any mishaps by an angry doe. (Does have been known to castrate a good buck in this fashion.) Try to keep the breeding as natural as possible and only interfere when necessary.

Breeding should be done in a quiet atmosphere. It is helpful to talk to the doe, calming and reassuring her and the buck. Unwilling does may be at the end of a cycle when old eggs are being absorbed and new eggs are being developed. Once stimulated, these does should be returned for service eight to ten hours later.

Breeding is best done early in the morning when the Lops are feeling their best and before the heat of the day. Breeding late at night with insufficient lighting can be risky when carrying around a frisky doe. Also, Lops are easily spooked at night and therefore prone to injury. I recommend that the buck service the doe two to three times at each breeding session. Refrain from using the same buck on more than one doe on the same day if the breeding is to be repeated eight to ten hours later. It takes about six hours after breeding for the semen to attain sufficient volume for successful breeding.

Teasing a pair of potential lovers that cannot get together within a reasonable period of time usually works out well. If the buck is not interested in the doe, take the doe away for a short while. Bring the doe to the buck again and again about eight hours later. If he still shows no interest, repeat the procedure daily. Before too long, he will take advantage of his brief visitor.

Restricting the doe (forced mating) results in a low conception rate. Restricting the doe after a play period with the buck increases the conception rate. The play period varies with individual Lops. For some it is a romance, while others play chase, and yet others may find a brawl more stimulating than the make-up period. Be careful that the buck is not intimidated or hurt by an overly aggressive doe who either wants no part of him or is demonstrative in showing him how it should be done at his expense. Pregnant does, those out of heat and those that believe they are pregnant may truly turn on the buck, turn tail and run, or tuck tail and cry.

A doe willingly accepting a buck will lift her tail to meet his advances. When contact has been made, the buck will fall away from the doe to one side, usually with a grunt, as if shot. Successful breedings have been known to occur without this ritual, so always mark the date of service, seemingly successful or not.

If a doe does not conceive after repeated breedings, you can contact your veterinarian to have the doe injected with a hormone to increase sexual activity. The sexual peak is 72 to 96 hours after the injection, but even then, there is a 50% chance the doe will respond.

Accurate records of the breedings on hutch cards or the like should be kept. The nest box should be given to the doe about five days before kindling. If a pregnant doe becomes too restless, throwing her crocks and sitting board about and digging frantically at the board or floor, give the nest box to her early to keep her busy and calm her. Crocks can be secured by wire crock hangers.

Do not place the nest box in a potty corner and make sure its backside or side protects the interior from the wind or any draft.

Count 31 days from the date bred to arrive at the due date for kindling. Lops can kindle as early as the 29th day and as late as the 33rd day. Kits born three days or more past the 31st day are usually born dead. Excitement, handling and other stressful conditions tend to prolong gestation. Therefore, it is imperative to give the doe oxytocin to induce labor by the 33rd day. This is obtained through a veterinarian. When given, be prepared to gather scattered kits on the floor as this takes the doe by surprise and encourages unnatural behavior. I recommend padding wire floors with straw or hay to reduce injury to the newborn kits.

If the doe pulls fur on the 17th or 18th day after breeding, she has gone through a false or pseudo pregnancy. In that case, she should be mated on the 17th or 18th day to conceive. Breeding a doe during a false pregnancy at this time is almost always a sure conception.

Palpating is considered the best way of testing for pregnancy. Two people may be necessary until you gain sufficient experience in the procedure. To palpate, restrain the doe on a table with one hand over the shoulders. Stretch the doe out with the other hand under her flank. The doe must be relaxed to palpate. Keeping fingers together, feel for the embryos between your thumb and fingers. There must be sufficient pressure to feel the individual fetal balls in the area behind the pelvic bone and high in the abdominal cavity. At ten to fourteen days, the embryos should feel like small grapes in line one-half to one inch apart. Palpation after the 17th day is difficult.

If not done properly, palpating can injure the doe and/or her growing embryos. Therefore, it is recommended to test the doe for pregnancy by returning her to the buck in ten days from breeding to see if she will accept or reject the buck. A pregnant doe usually will run away, crouch down and cry, with the last resort being an attack on the buck. There are exceptions to this rule.

I usually find myself watching the behavior pattern of the doe. A pregnant doe will lie down more often the closer she comes to kindling and will go off her feed a few days prior to kindling. Movement in her abdominal area can be seen during the last few days. Do not confuse the rippling, flowing movement of digestion with the definite pops or kicks of the kits. Pops are babies!

Breeding

Proper feed is very important to the pregnant doe. High protein rabbit pellets are a must. Calf Manna, Manamar or Stock Builder should be added (one teaspoon to one tablespoon) to bring about milk for the babies. Good alfalfa hay added to the diet will keep the doe eating when her appetite decreases just before kindling. It is wise not to move a doe to another cage or transport her to a new location after two weeks into her pregnancy, especially if this is her first pregnancy.

Psychological and physical stress from poor sanitation, inadequate food or water supply, crowding, fumes from ammonia (urine), paint or insecticide fumes, or an intimidating buck can cause resorption of young and lower resistance to disease.

Normally there is a definite change in the personality of a pregnant doe. More often than not she will be edgy. It is important not to provoke the doe but to give her peace, quiet and love during this stressful period. I provide soothing FM music in the rabbitry during kindling and storms as well as on a daily basis. Soothing music really calms the savage beast, as well as the Lops, during stressful times. After the doe kindles and builds trust in you, she will become more personable and dependent on you. I have seen the most impersonal doe turn into Miss Congeniality after motherhood.

Bucks should not be allowed with the does before, at or after kindling. Once pregnant, the doe regards the buck as her worst enemy and will destroy her young out of love, to protect them rather than have them destroyed by the buck.

NURSERY

Pregnant does should be alone in large cages with babysaver wire and a doorway large enough to accommodate a large nest box. Six foot cages are recommended for the English and French does, five foot cages are recommended for the Mini does and three foot cages are recommended for the Holland does.

Wooden nest boxes are preferable to metal ones because they can be made large enough and the wood does not conduct the heat and cold like metal. Many babies have been lost due to roasting in the summer, freezing in the winter or being squashed along the sides or in the corners of metal nest boxes.

Nest box dimensions are as follows:

English and French Lops—24 inches in length, 7 inches high at the foot, 12 inches high at the head, 15 inches wide, and an 11-inch top or bonnet at the head to prevent the doe from jumping directly on her babies. The floor should have holes drilled it at regular intervals for proper drainage. Drill the holes before assembling the box to keep the rough edges on the outside. I use CDX ¾ inch plywood since it is more finished and smooth.

Mini Lops—20 inches in length, 6 inches high at the foot, 11 inches high at the head, 11 inches wide, and a 9-inch top or bonnet at the head. The floor should be as above for the English and French.

Holland Lops—14 inches in length, 4 inches high at the foot, 9 inches high at the head, 8 inches wide, and a 6-inch top or bonnet at the head, or larger, to accommodate a nest box warmer which is a plate 17 inches by 9 inches (18 inches long by 10½ inches wide).

Pack the bottom of the nest box with straw and top with a layer of hay. The hay is not only nutritional for the babies but will help prevent the loss of kits in large pockets created by the bulky straw. Mulched straw is ideal to use, but if not available, a closely-woven bedding can be made using hay over the straw. Do not use sawdust or any other dusty material for bedding as this can induce respiratory and eye problems.

Kindling

Sometimes kindling or giving birth takes the first-time mother by surprise and usually takes about 30 minutes. I have literally followed an expectant doe around with a nest box, constantly cleaning out her droppings and urine. The day before kindling, I had to reposition her nesting material and fur in the nest box because she placed it on the wire in a corner. Finally, she realized what the nest box was for only minutes before giving birth.

Does usually pull fur just before kindling, but there are exceptions. There are times you will have to pull fur from a doe to give sufficient cover for the newborn babies or kittens. With birth comes a loosening of fur around the dewlap and rump for this purpose.

It is best to be nearby at the time of kindling as does do not pick up any kits stranded on the wire and place them safely in the nest box. Lops still have the primitive instincts of the wild rabbit whose kits can crawl along the ground and drop safely into the hole or nest. Babies caught on the wire for any length of time will eventually lose body heat to the point of death. Also, legs may be damaged by hanging through the wire with a resultant loss of circulation. Does have been known to panic if taken by surprise with crying newborns on the wire, sometimes trampling them or devouring them to save them from their distress. If this be the case, remove the nest box and kits from the doe and quickly make up the nest box like it should be. Give the doe back her babies along with a treat, once she has settled down.

Does may leave babies suffocating in afterbirth or in rare cases begin devouring them because of some disturbance. Distract the doe by speaking softly to her and giving her a treat while rescuing the kits. It is best to remove the nest box entirely for a brief period than to work within the cage with the chance of the doe jumping into the nest box unexpectedly. Also, you can take the kits away to a safe, warm place and leave the nest box in the cage until the doe settles down and looks for her babies. Then give them back to her when she is calm and settled in the nest box.

There are times a cold, lifeless baby can be brought back to life if submerged in warm water from the shoulders down while massaging the body. Loss of body heat seems to bring about a dormant state that eventually passes into death.

A doe in labor will not eat her most favorite treat or clean herself thoroughly until after kindling. I use a banana as a barometer to tell me if she is about to kindle, when she is done or if there is a problem.

Encourage does to eat and drink, in order to guarantee the milk needed, by treating them to fresh fruits especially bananas and vegetables, such as celery that has sodium to make does thirsty, and giving a crock of flavored gelatin in water. I find Strawberry/Banana Jello a favorite, though some like apple juice. Prepare the Jello water by using cold water and adding enough Jello to taste and smell good, stirring well. The Jello will settle quite a bit at the bottom by the end of the day. Replace it with a fresh mixture daily. I find the Jello water accepted by most does and have brought through more kits because of more milk produced by it. Be careful not to draw ants with the Jello water. I apply livestock fly spray or place a band of Tree Tanglefoot around each leg of the hutch to stop any climbing insects. Apple juice plus a small amount of water can be placed in a water bottle, but must be changed daily.

KINDLING PROBLEMS

I truly believe in bioclimatic relationships affecting conception, kindling, and the like.

Prolapsed uterus is rare, but has been known to happen for no apparent reason apart from an overdose of oxytocin. The uterus comes out, or is expelled, with the babies. I have seen this happen to two large French Lop does, a bloody, messy sight. It is possible to save the doe and possibly the babies too if action is taken immediately. Surgery by a veterinarian usually results in a spay. The babies are best fostered to other does as surgery leaves the doe in a weakened condition with no appetite and no milk for the kits. A lot of love, personal attention, hand feeding of grapes, bananas, Nutri-Cal, and Jello water will save the doe. Chloromycetin Palmitate given orally for at least ten days and Nitrofurazone ointment applied daily to the sutured area are the medications used to prevent infection.

Overcleaning of the young is rare but it does happen. A difficult kindling may cause a doe to stress to the point of overcleaning her young at birth, resulting in eaten extremities such as tails and ears. If this happens, give the doe another chance, making sure she is kept trim to avoid difficult labor. I find the doe can also be diverted with special treats during kindling, thereby giving her something else to eat.

Rejection of young by a doe may be because she instinctively knows something is physically wrong with the kits. Does have been known to separate problem kits from others in the nest by continuously placing them in a far corner of the nest box. If the same kit or kits are repeatedly found away from the nest, it may mean mother knows best and is culling her litter.

Rejection of young by a doe is also obvious when the tummies of the kits are not full of milk and appear shriveled or dehydrated. Also, the kits will jump about and cry when touched if they are hungry. Sometimes a doe becomes depressed to the point of not eating or caring for her litter. This may be due to lack of her physical fitness or a stressful environment such as too small a cage or nest box. If a doe believes she cannot successfully raise her litter in a good environment, she may reject them. This was proven by a large French Lop doe who would not readily conceive and rejected her litter when she kindled in a four foot cage. This so-called bad, temperamental, nasty mother was relocated to a six foot cage where she successfully kindled and raised litters with affectionate care.

If a doe manages to raise her litter in crowded conditions, she may wean them very early and eventually turn on them because of the never-ending stressful situation.

If after 24 hours there are babies in need of milk, put on a long-sleeved jacket or shirt for protection and remove the nest box and babies from the cage. Place the nest box on a table in view, and return for the doe. If there are many kits the same color, the use of another appropriate container to segregate those kits which have already nursed is handy. Take one baby at a time and let it nurse on each nipple. Start with the stronger babies as they will pull the milk to the surface for the weaker ones. The doe has eight nipples, with the upper pair located between the front legs. The kit will travel from nipple to nipple and eventually settle down to a couple of favorites. This behavior of kits is a survival instinct which allows each his fair share of the milk supply. I have saved litters this way. After three days, one doe jumped in to feed her litter on schedule when she saw me coming. A Grand Champion buck exists today because of hand or manual feeding—initially, he was the only one left out at dinner time, but not in the end. Does do not stay with their young like canine bitches do to guarantee that everyone gets a good meal. Therefore, it is important that she has milk for the young for the times she hovers over them in the nest box, usually once in the morning and once at night.

Supplemental feedings can be given to a doe who is totally off feed by using a syringe filled with a mixture of soybean-based baby formula, high protein baby cereal and Nutri-Cal.

Such feedings can be given to the young, using a soybean-based baby formula with a touch of Nutri-Cal or light corn syrup and protein powder or using a kitten formula with added bone meal. An eye dropper, pet nursing bottle or small syringe can be used to feed the kits, but be sure to give a small amount very often, avoiding overdosing (milk coming out of the nose) which can result in death due to fluid in the lungs. Usually kits cannot be raised totally in this fashion devoid of doe's milk for which there is not an adequate substitute. Kits appear malnourished regardless of the intake of formula and may appear to have abnormally large heads in comparison to body size, among other deformities such as rickets, when several weeks of age. Use of a stomach tube to feed babies is so traumatic for the fragile kits that it has proven unsuccessful. When hand feeding, do remember to wipe the genital area of the babies after feeding using a warm moist cotton ball to encourage urination and defecation.

The best insurance policy is to have a backup doe for fostering babies. By breeding more than one doe at a time, you can foster babies born within three days of one another. Care should be taken to clean off any of the original doe's fur that may be attached to the baby being fostered and place the kit at the bottom of the litter in the new nest box in order to acquire the scent of the new littermates. If in doubt about the doe's acceptance of the fostered babies, put a touch of vanilla extract on each baby and on the doe's nose and *you* will feel better.

I do not recommend keeping other breeds of rabbits strictly for nurse does for the Lops. I have tried this and the outcome was more cage space taken, more time expended, skittish fostered Lop babies and the necessary destruction of the nurse doe's babies (a feeling I never want to experience again). Additionally, there is the loss of a quality that should be imprinted in the Lops—the ability to successfully care for young.

Dead newborn kits strewn about the cage and nest box may be an indication of predators or unusual noises frightening the doe. Large babies are sometimes found dead because of problems incurred by the doe in passing them. Bruises and torn areas on the bodies of the babies are signs that the doe did have problems during delivery. Sometimes a doe will make her nest at the front of the nest box and unintentionally squash babies with her body when hopping in and out. Squashed kits have blood in the nails and a bitten tongue. It is important to keep the nest under the bonnet of the nest box in order to protect the kits from this mishap. Should something spook the doe, causing her to dash into the nest box, chances are the litter will be safe under the bonnet.

The sudden death of healthy, well-fed kits five to seven days old may mean Milk Enterotoxemia, which is common in the mid-western section of the United States. The cause of this condition is the overgrowth in the milk of a bacteria that produces a toxin causing sudden death. Excessive milk production when kits are over ten days of age does not cause a problem. Should this occur, limitation of the total energy intake (feed) of the doe just 24 hours prior to and 72 hours immediately following kindling will prevent this from happening again. Milk is richest at the start of lactation and production is at its peak the third and fourth week after kindling, slowly declining thereafter.

Another cause of sudden death of kits may be extreme temperatures. It is important that the nest box be kept dry. In very cold climates, a nest box warmer, which is a 20-watt waterproof heat cable embedded between two steel plates 17 inches by 9 inches, may be imperative. It is possible to remove a nest box of newborns to be kept in a safe, protected area such as your house, and return it to the doe for short periods of time in the morning and in the evening for nursing. This has been successfully done during extreme hot spells. During the heat spells, be sure also to push the fur away from the litter to prevent heat prostration and recover the kits when the temperature cools off.

Kindling

The problem of a doe urinating on the litter can be prevented by completely removing the nest box of kits from the doe and returning it and the kits clean and dry to her for short periods of time in the morning and evening for nursing. When the kits become older, the doe will most likely stop this lazy, bad habit and be allowed to keep her babies with her. An excellent place to keep a nest box full of kits is in a bathroom in a bathtub, with the door closed to keep them safe from other household pets.

Abortion or loss of a litter at kindling is mourned by a doe. It is best to breed her again three days or 72 hours later if good physical condition permits.

Giant dead kits sometimes born to does who have successfully raised one or more normal-sized litters are a physiological disorder. It occurs when a small number of fetuses are present and receive abundant nutrition from the uterine blood supply. This enlarges them to abnormal size over a lengthened gestation period. The kits are usually born dead and kindling is difficult for the does. This generally does not affect the succeeding litters.

Cannibalism of young is rare but is sometimes the result of a difficult birth, an unusually nervous doe, abnormal development of the young, abnormal noises, predators, strangers, poor diet, deprivation of water, or dehydration of the doe. For example, a pregnant French Lop doe consumes about one-half gallon of fresh water per day.

Mastitis is a bacterial infection (abscess) of the mammary gland, and causes a doe to refuse to nurse her previously cared for young. The infection can spread throughout the doe's system and releases fatal toxins in the milk. The doe's temperature may rise to 105°F and she will crave water. The abscess should be treated and possibly surgically removed by a veterinarian, and the doe medicated, using Chloromycetin Palmitate orally for ten days. (See abscess care in the Health Chapter.)

Death of the doe a day or two before or at kindling is

Kindling

usually due to Ketosis (pregnancy toxemia). This is a rare disorder that may affect an obese doe or one not physically fit, due to lack of exercise.

Nest box mortality at three days of age may be the result of Metritis (infection of the uterus) following kindling. The doe lactates and then ceases to milk, due to toxemia produced by bacteria within the uterus. The young are healthy for the first 24 hours and then dehydrate rapidly and usually die about the third day due to dehydration and starvation. Usually there is a 100 percent mortality and there may be signs of scours in the babies. There is no vaginal discharge to be seen, only the mortality of the young at three to four days. See your veterinarian for treatment.

At kindling a hernia may appear on the stomach of a doe. This is caused by a rupture affecting the intestines and causing a blockage. This condition requires immediate veterinarian care to prevent death of the doe who may be carrying unborn kits but is unable to expel them due to a painful, weakened condition. If the blockage is not surgically corrected, the doe will die in acute pain because of accumulated intestinal matter and toxic gases.

Timely recognition of and response to abnormal behavior is the key to finding and successfully treating a problem.

Care of Mother and Young

Soothing words and a treat in a quiet atmosphere will reassure the doe there is nothing to fear as you help care for her and her babies. Daily checking of babies is no problem when done properly.

Always check the doe for symptoms of a chronic wet dewlap and fungal infection because of the increase of her water intake. Treat as instructed in the Health chapter. An untreated wet dewlap will spread and abscess and may bring on respiratory problems in cold weather.

Care of Mother and Young

Check for babies that may not be getting enough milk. These babies will be thin and the flank area will be sunken rather than rounded. Hungry babies will be very irritable when touched and squeal from hunger. These babies do not last for more than two or three days, so it is imperative that supplemental feedings commence immediately, preferably by using the doe herself, as outlined in the section on Kindling Problems.

Make sure that the nest box is kept very clean to prevent skin and eye infections. Check daily the number of young and make sure they are together and not stranded in or out of the nest box. Hungry kits can accidentally ride out on the doe's nipple. Therefore, it is important to keep a good amount of hay on the sitting board at the base of the nest box to offer some protection to a kit in trouble. Later this will serve as food and as a cushion and protection for their legs when the kits start jumping out of the nest box.

Remove any dead babies, afterbirth not consumed by the doe and any dirty bedding immediately after kindling. Wash the doe and the sitting board if either are bloody or soiled. Every two to three days, remove the nest box and the babies from the cage and place them on a table. Give the doe a treat so she will not get nervous. Using a sanitary, appropriate container, place the kits and clean fur in the container while you dump the bedding from the nest box. I use a large, plastic container, putting paper toweling at the bottom to absorb any urine and add straw or hay in cold weather for insulation. This is cleaned out with each usage. Wipe dry the bottom of the nest box with paper toweling should there be urine. Place new bedding in the nest box. I place a layer of straw at the bottom and then a fine layer of alfalfa hay and its leaves to eliminate large pockets usually created by straw if not mulched and to allow food for the young when of age. Form a pocket for the babies under the bonnet and replace the doe's fur and the babies. If more fur is needed, pull it from around the dewlap and haunches of the doe.

Also, take time to examine each baby, making sure there are no abscesses around the genital area or other parts of the body and no tears or wounds.

If abscesses are found, sometimes seen where the scent glands are located on either side of the genitalia, open them with a sterile needle, flush clean with hydrogen peroxide and apply Nitrofurazone ointment or liquid daily till healed. Keep a separate needle for each litter and rinse with alcohol and store in a shot glass in a water and Betadine solution until no longer needed; then discard it. See Health chapter for abscess treatment.

Wounds or tears can be safely cleaned with hydrogen peroxide and coated with Nitrofurazone ointment daily till healed.

The kits are blind and deaf until ten days of age. Slower maturing kits will take a day or two longer to be able to see. Should an eye or both eyes fail to open after a reasonable length of time, a bacterial infection may be suspected. Do not force the eyes open if they do not open when gentle pressure is applied. Instead, wipe the eyes gently with a moist, sterile piece of cotton using an eye wash such as a boric acid solution until it or they open. If the eye continues to seal shut the next day, repeat the treatment and apply a small amount of Terramycin eye ointment daily until it is no longer needed, usually within seven days.

When the eyes open, place some pellets and some crimped oats or dry old fashioned oatmeal in the nest box to introduce the kits to a solid diet. Introduction of a rabbit pellet specifically designed for babies or a creep feed is desirable.

Sexing the babies can be done at close to three weeks of age. Hold the kit on its back. While placing your thumbs above the genital area and, moving the skin upward, pull the tail back and down between the first and second fingers. The buck's genitalia will protrude upward like a donut, while the doe's genitalia will form a slit, protruding upward toward the upper body and declining and connecting at the rectum. Late blooming bucks have been mistaken for does at about two months of age, so it is a good idea to recheck the Lops as they grow older.

Dirty nest boxes will result in acute staph infections (abscesses), and possibly maggot or ant infestation. If the floor of the nest box must be washed, do so with a bleach and water solution, rinse with water and dry it thoroughly using a portable hand hair dryer before replacing the nesting material and babies.

Because bacteria and nest boxes go hand in hand, nest boxes should be removed when the babies are three weeks of age. Before that time, the kits may be coming out of the nest box after the mother, possibly because of insufficient lactation. If the kits seem to relish the security of the nest box and do not seem as mature at three weeks, perhaps due to many littermates or insufficient lactation, let them keep the nest box until such time as they start venturing out on their own. Remember, rules of thumb vary with individual situations, so act in the best interest of the kits. Lops are made or broken in the nursery.

Before storing it, disinfect a nest box with bleach and water (1 part bleach to 10 parts water) using a large brush, rinse well with water and set in the sun to dry. Store in a clean, dry place free from contamination by insects and/or rodents. Disease-causing bacteria can be passed from one generation to the next via the nest box without proper disinfection and sanitation.

In wire floor cages, place a sitting board in the place of the nest box and add a mound of hay on top for the kits to eat and cuddle in now that the nest box is gone. Weather and age permitting, the kits will no longer need a nest of hay. Be sure to protect them from direct wind or draft by dropping tarps or the like on the sides of the cage.

Hang a # 1 crock in the cage for each kit plus one for the mother. This eliminates the problem of weaker, timid

Care of Mother and Young

babies becoming runts because of intimidation by the stronger ones. Allow space between crocks for kits. Also hang one or more water bottles low for backup should the water supply in the crock be insufficient. As the kits grow, an additional large water crock should be placed in the cage or check and refill the water crock more than once a day. If a doe has a large crock for food, it is wise to replace it with a # 1 crock to prevent the kits from sitting in the bowl and contaminating the feed with urine which in turn promotes infections of the genitalia. If a Jello and water solution has been given the doe, it should be removed and not given to the litter.

A pinch of Calf Manna, Manamar, Stock Builder or similar product should be added to the regular rabbit pellets in each bowl and continued if the feces of the babies remain firm. A tablespoon or more of a creep feed can be added to the regular rabbit pellets, if available.

Always check the babies' bottoms to make sure there is no diarrhea or fecal matter stopping the vents. If there is, wash with a mild soap (LOC, Basic H or castile soap), rinse well and dry and apply Nitrofurazone ointment should there be an irritation. Repeat daily until the area heals.

If there is acute diarrhea, remove additives, chlorinate the water and feed hay. If it persists, remove all pellets and feed straight hay until the condition subsides. Neomycin Sulfate Antidiarrheal Liquid can be administered, as explained in the Health chapter.

Check teeth and bites of the litter periodically, starting about three weeks of age, to make sure they have the proper overbite. If there seems to be malocclusion, use small wire cutters every couple of days to cut the teeth in the hope that with time and more skeletal growth, the upper jaw will lengthen to create the proper overbite. See the Grooming chapter for treatment of malocclusion and the possible cause in the Breeding Programs chapter.

Lop ears go through various growth stages: small tabs on

Weaning

each side of the head at birth, standing straight up or erect with growth, lengthening and dropping out to the side (airplane ears), both laying over to one side and then another, and then both down. A very narrow crown usually accompanied by a wide face will cause poor ear carriage, but Lop ears are down usually by seven or eight weeks of age. Slower maturing Lops like the Holland Lops may take up to three months for the ears to set properly.

Weaning

Seven-week-old litters are ready to be sent to new homes or weaned. There are times when a lazy mother will not have much control over her litter and a couple of kits may scrap at an early age of six weeks. The kits involved in such rough play should be removed from the litter and maintained in separate cages. There are times you may not see any fighting, but evidence of it is obvious when tufts of fur are seen in the cage and/or on the ground surrounding the cage. Close examination of the litter should disclose the culprits. Usually the ears are the first to be bitten and should be closely examined and treated if necessary.

There is a definite transition from mother to people from the sixth week to the seventh week and at that age the kits are most impressionable and ready to bond to people. There are times when a young Lop is adopted and placed in a new home at six and one-half weeks of age, but he definitely should not leave any younger, as this is detrimental to the physical and psychological well-being of the Lop.

Babies should gradually be weaned from the doe, making sure one lingers with her long enough to prevent her from developing caked breasts and to ease the end of lactation and dissolve her bond to her litter. Does will mourn loss of their litters. I had one French Lop doe who became grumpy and urinated on her sitting board constantly until bred again and proved happiest with her babies surrounding her.

Weaning

A doe can be kept with her young for a longer period of time, but make sure the bucks are removed from the does when they are three months of age to prevent inbreeding to their mother or sisters. Female littermates have been known to mount one another in play when older, but it is a good idea to recheck the sex at this point to make sure a late-blooming buck is not among them.

As a breeder, make it a point to sell directly to the public without a middleman, as your personal care, knowledge, help and information to the buyers after the sale plays an important role in the Lop's destiny.

Rebreeding the Doe

A doe in good condition can produce a maximum of four litters a year. Check the doe's breasts to make sure she is free from mastitis or any abscesses. Make sure that the doe is in good condition and not too thin or molting. Do not rebreed a doe with a litter still nursing. This is extremely hard on the doe, and it is not fair to stress her health to a possible breaking point. You cannot breed the Lops like commercial rabbits without jeopardizing their physical and mental health. They are sensitive, and it is this sensitivity that makes them great pets.

Please remember that Lop rabbits are not to be treated on the same basis as commercial rabbits; this is a great injustice to the Lops, who give their all to reproduce themselves, even to the point of death.

Tattooing

Tattooing is a permanent form of identification in the left ear which is done by the breeder of pedigreed Lop rabbits. A small animal tattoo kit with a set of numbers and letters and tattoo ink can be purchased. The tattoo pliers hold five metal or plastic digits 5/16 inch high. The system for identification can be whatever the breeder wants to use to identify the Lops in a breeding program.

I use the doe's initials and the buck's initials, and then number according to litter number of the respective breeding pair and use a second number to designate the number given within the litter. For example: Raisin and Punch's first baby's ear to be tattooed from their first litter together would read, "RP11." The first baby's ear to be tattooed in their second litter together would read, "RP21."

Tattoo between five and a half and six weeks of age so that the ear is healed before the litter is sold and before the ears thicken with age. Take this time to check teeth, ears, straightness of legs, sex and body type of the litter. I recommend having an assistant to help tattoo, placing the litter to be tattooed in a carrier and working on a large table in a well-lit area. Check over the first baby to be tattooed and make notes of the ear number assigned, sex, color, and good body type. Look for good curvature of spine, width of chest and spring of front rib and good width between hind legs or heels and note accordingly. Look for a wide rear end because good shoulder development will slowly follow. Flatness or length of shoulder at this age most likely will not disappear at maturity. I find that body type of my French Lops at this age is an indication of what they will be at maturity. The growth stages which follow are very misleading of the worth of a Lop on the show table. Selection for body type in the Holland Lop is usually made at four weeks; thereafter, the Hollands appear rangy and/or out of proportion until maturity.

When you begin to tattoo, sit at the table with your assistant seated to your right, holding the first baby firmly on the table and against his or her chest for support. Wipe the left ear with a cotton ball moistened with alcohol to remove dirt and wax buildup. Arrange the number and letters in the pliers and on a piece of paper test to see if they read right and make an even impression. Hold the left ear up to the light to find a spot devoid of any large veins, position the ear in the pliers and clamp down on the spot quickly and firmly, releasing quickly. Brush tattooing ink mixed with a little India ink quickly over the impression, filling in the holes. Follow up by rubbing the area firmly with your thumb and/or brushing further with a small, fine toothbrush. Allow the ink to dry in the ear and the excess to wear away naturally with time.

Tattooing is similar to ear piercing and when done properly is quick and soon forgotten by the Lop. If by chance a vein is hit or the impression goes through the ear, profuse bleeding can be stopped by using Kwik Stop or other blood clotting antiseptic powder or styptic pencil. Always disinfect the letters and numbers between animals by using alcohol, most convenient and sanitary in a spray bottle. Infected ears can easily result from unsanitary equipment.

The right ear is reserved for a registration number should the Lop be registered by an official Registrar of the American Rabbit Breeders Association. This is a requirement before one can officially record a Grand Champion with the ARBA.

To qualify for registration, a purebred Lop does not have to have both parents registered, but does need a three-generation pedigree. The ancestors listed on the pedigree can be registered, out of registered animals or not registered at all, but of the same breed. A registered Lop is one that has met all technical and physical qualifications, has been approved by a licensed ARBA Registrar and recorded permanently by a tattoo in the right ear, which is officially recorded and kept on file by the ARBA. A registered Lop is free of physical disqualifications and eliminations, and is of the desired senior weight when registered.

Registrars are found at rabbit shows or can be contacted at home by using the ARBA Yearbook for guidance in finding one in your area. Registrars will allow use of your own tattooing equipment in their presence should you so desire. I recommend not using a tattoo box for holding rabbits to be tattooed as this is a frightening experience that has resulted in a broken back or similar mishap for a few.

Tattoo numbers must be legible if the Lop is to be shown. A hand needle for touch up can be used should the ear number be illegible. A Registrar will often have such a tool and for a nominal fee, will be more than happy to correct an unreadable tattoo.

Ear tattoos on the English Lop must be in the upper edge of the ear not visible when posed. This is just under the edge of the cartilage which forms the roll of the upper ear (approximately three to four inches from the head on a senior) thus made visible only by lifting the ear and rolling it gently toward you.

Pedigrees

A pedigree is a three-generation record of the ancestry of a Lop and is made up by the breeder for a litter when both parents of the same breed are pedigreed. The pedigree ear number should correspond to that number tattooed in the left ear. Pedigree information is filled in and attested to by the breeder to the best of his or her knowledge and belief. Each pedigreed Lop should have his own pedigree paper signed by the breeder, identifying sex, color, tattoo number and ancestry, and sold with the Lop or kept on file by the breeder with a purchase option by the buyer at a later date. It is important to keep copies of all pedigree papers even after death and sale as this will provide information for breeding programs and duplicate pedigree papers if needed.

Forms can be obtained for a small fee through the American Rabbit Breeders Association and some national and local breed clubs. A breeder may wish to have his own personal pedigree forms printed using the ARBA format as a guide, thereby allowing more space for additional information.

Shipping

When faced with shipping rabbits via air freight, you will find, after talking to different airline personnel even within the same airline, that it is most confusing and has been a most discouraging endeavor for years. Many airlines assume rabbits are shipped like dogs in flight kennels, and health certificates are required. Though dealing with a domestic rabbit, unlike dogs and cats, the rabbit is not allowed onboard with the passenger as it is not considered by the airlines to be a domestic animal. Therefore, you are looking at shipping air freight.

Flight kennels are strong, guaranteed safe, made of sanitary poly-plastic, have draft-free ventilation and are accepted by all airlines. They are great for dogs, but not for rabbits. The slick floor can very easily turn into a skating rink during transport, resulting in broken bones, and the draft-free walls restrict the much-needed air flow for the furry, stressing animals.

Keven Whaley (KW Cages) and I, therefore, pooled our knowledge of rabbits and cages, resulting in an airline-approved rabbit flight carrier. The flight carrier has been successfully and safely used for the past few years by me and other breeders and pet owners to ship the Lops.

The flight carrier is 16 inches deep, 24 inches long and 14 inches high and made out of $\frac{1}{2}$ inch by 1 inch heavy wire. There are a doubled wire divider, carrying handles, safety-latched top and bottom paper tray, flight information card holder, and a removable, galvanized steel top plate which is inserted or removed according to various airline regulations. Dimensions fall within minimum freight charge.

The carrier is divided lengthwise to accommodate two Lops. The divider is kept intact when shipping only one, with the Lop on one side and a sealed can of transition food on the other, thus minimizing jostle. It is highly recommended to ship rabbits in pairs, minimum age being three months, to reduce stress.

When shipping two Lops, two sealed one-pound coffee cans of transition food should be wired in opposite corners on either side of the divider to distribute the weight evenly. When shipping in hot weather, one-quart milk cartons with tops removed, frozen with water also should be wired in opposite corners. These function as air-conditioners and a continuous supply of cold water. In addition, it is recommended that a carrot for each Lop be placed in the carrier for moisture and pacification.

Flight information, consignee's name, address and phone number, shipper's name, address and phone number, and any special instructions should be written on a card and taped in the card holder with transparent tape to secure and protect the card.

I have found that United Airlines is very good to deal with and require a minimum 24-hour notice before flight. They also require the Lops be at the freight office at least 1½ hours before takeoff. Two copies of a health certificate from your veterinarian are needed, dated within ten days of shipment.

It is wise for a breeder to have the Lops, health certificates and carrier paid for in advance by the consignee, leaving the air-freight bill, including insurance, to be paid C.O.D. A collect, long-distance phone call made to the consignee is important soon after the Lops are in flight to verify arrival time, etc., and most important, to relay the airbill number.

Though it is desirable to have a direct, nonstop flight, sometimes circumstances warrant a stopover or change of planes. Both the shipper and consignee can monitor the shipment by calling the airlines, requesting the status by giving the airbill number which is fed into a computer. United has temperature-controlled, animal retaining rooms to house the Lops between flights or until pickup. I always request the consignee to call me as soon as possible after pickup to let me know the Lops are safe and well and to allow me to answer any last-minute questions.

After use, the flight carrier adapts to a practical, useful carrying cage by simply removing the divider and, if used, the steel top plate. Consequently, the consignee finds the purchase of the flight carrier a worthwhile investment in a very useful piece of equipment.

Zoning Regulations

Recently, with the population growth and the establishment of city ordinances, the hobbyist who breeds the Fancy/Pet rabbit has been winning the battle against being zoned out like the commercial meat and fur rabbit breeder has been.

City government officials are receiving an education on the Lop rabbit, the King of the Fancy, the Pet and the important role it plays in society. Locally, the Lop/Fancy rabbit breeder has received more concessions than the local kennel, mainly because of the noise factor. I raise the French Lops under the same governing policies and beliefs as I raise my dogs and horses, devoid of butchering, slaughter and insensitive culling solely to a winner on the show table. The Lops are winners of the heart, "soul" food, accepting and loving people for what they are with the hope of its devotion being returned. It was with great pride that I admitted this at a City Council Zoning Hearing, explaining the role of the floppy-eared therapist/companion animal and his contribution to community service.

I shared the same victory recently won by Lop breeders in Ontario, Canada, who proved with much pride that there is the dedicated "pet" rabbit breeder who puts his animals before himself without slaughter. As one Canadian breeder stated to an official, "You be the one to tell my daughter (who is handicapped) which ones have to go! I cannot!"

INDEX

Abscesses, 122
Alfalfa hay, 68
American Lop Club, 37
American Pet Show, 6
American Rabbit Breeders
    Association, 39, 42, 45, 47, 49,
    104, 107
Appetite, abnormal, 120
Apples, 74
Bananas, 74
Barley, 74
Behavior, abnormal, 120
Best Opposite Sex, defined, 108
Best Opposite Sex of Variety,
    defined, 108
Best of Breed, defined, 108
Best of Variety, defined, 108
Bloody urine, 119
Bloomers, 41
Book of the Lop, 37
British Rabbit Council, 39, 42,
    45, 49, 107
Brooks, Aleck, 47
Cabbage, 74
Cage size, 58
Carbohydrates, 68
Castration, 99
Celery, 74
Chatham and Rochester Fancy
    Rabbit Club, 35
Chief Sealth 8
Chinchilla rabbit, 44
Coccidiosis, 66, 115
Conjunctivitis, 130
Corn on the cob, 74
Cuterebra larvae, 130
Dandruff, 128

Delta Society, 6, 30
Diet, 66-76
Dust ruffles, 41
Ears, grooming, 78-82
English Lop, 35, 39
Enteritis, 66, 58, 68
Entropion, 130
Eye irritations, treatment for, 82
Eyes, weepy, 126, 128
FEAT program, 24
Flat Lop, 35
Flemish Giant, 35, 40
Fogger system, 134
French Lop, 40-43
Fruit juices, 74
Fur chewing, 132
German Big Lop, 44
Grand Champion Certificate, 109
Grooming, 78-88
Half Lop, 35
Harnessbreaking, 102
Hay, 68, 68
Hay cubes, 70
Head-down disease, 121
Health problems, external, 122
Health problems, internal, 113-
    121
Heat prostration, 134
Herschbach, Bob, 44
Holland Lop, 47
Holland Lop Rabbit Specialty
    Club, 47
Horned Lop, 35
Housebreaking, 90-101
Housing accessories, 63
Housing, indoor, 62
Housing, outdoor, 56

Hutch burn, 122
Hutch disinfection, 80
Hutches, 64
Jaeggi, Herman, 40
Kindling cages, 58
Kites, Lops' reaction to, 14
Klein Widder, 44
Lockley, R.M., 14
London Fancy Rabbit Society, 36
Lop Rabbit Club of America, 6
Maggot infestation, 136
McQueen, Steve, 22
Meisel, Bunnye, 103
Mickewitx, B.J., 37
Milkweed, 68
Mini Lop, 44-46
Mites, 78, 127
Molting, 86-88
Movement, abnormal, 121
Mucoid enteritis, 116
Nails, caring for, 84
National Lop Club of Great
    Britain, 37
Natural Lop, 35
Netherland Dwarf Lop, 47
Night feces, 74
Normandy Giant, 40
Oar Lop, 35
Oat groats, 74
Oat hay, 68
Oats, 74
Oranges, 74
Paralysis, 121
Pasteurella, 36, 110 , 117
Pasteurella Multocida, 118
Pasteurellosis, 117

PETE program, 30
Pedigree papers, 105
Pellets, 66
Pneumonia, 36
Poisonous plants, 74
Rolled corn, 74
Salt spools, 72
San Diego County Lop Breeders
    Association, 6
Sharp Hospital Rehabilitation
    Center, 33
Showing, 104-110
Sneezing, 117
Snuffles, 36, 117
Spaying, 99
Splay legs, 132
Spraddle legs, 132
Spraying of urine, 99
Starch, 68
Stress, 58, 115
Sulfa drugs, 115
Sunflower seeds, 74
Sweepstakes Point System, 109
Syphilis, 138
Tapeworms, 66
Teeth, caring for, 82-84
Transportation equipment, 105
Tricks, 102
Trousers, 41
Van de Cock, Adrian, 47
Vent disease, 138
Vitamins, 72
Water, 72
Wet dewlap, 125
White, Ken 30